RAGE!
REFLECT.
REJOICE!

DATE DUE

RAGE! REFLECT. REJOICE!

PRAYING WITH THE PSALMISTS

Thomas H. Troeger

The Westminster Press
Philadelphia

Scripture quotations from the Revised Standard Version of the Bible are
copyrighted 1946, 1952, © 1971, 1973 by the Division of Christian Educa-
tion of the National Council of the Churches of Christ in the U.S.A, and
are used by permission.

First edition

Published by The Westminster Press ®
Philadelphia, Pennsylvania

Printed in the United States of America

9 8 7 6 5 4 3 2 1

To R.L.M.
whose clear and candid
questions
drove me to write this book

Library of Congress Cataloging in Publication Data

Troeger, Thomas H   1945–
   Rage! Reflect. Rejoice!

   1. Prayer. 2. Bible. O.T. Psalms—Criticism,
interpretation, etc. I. Title.
BV210.2.T76   248'.3   77–22755
ISBN 0–664–24293–6

Contents

Continued

Introduction

How can I start to pray?

How can I understand the psalms?

These questions are frequently joined together because people who are trying to shape a devotional life often turn to reading a psalm. They sense that the psalms are about prayer but are baffled by the style and language. This book tries to untangle these difficulties and to show how the psalms instruct us in praying from common experience.

Pious twaddle is the booby trap of devotional literature. If I have fallen into it, the fault is my own and not the psalmists' nor the many people whose stories fill this book.

I am grateful to those ancient Israelites who spoke to God with fierce directness and to those modern persons who were honest enough to say to me, "I don't have any idea how to pray." If this book is in any way faithful to the psalmists and helpful to those seeking God's personal presence, then I shall be glad indeed.

T.H.T.

1

Exactly How I Feel

That's exactly how I feel! I have not been able to say it, but you've put it in just the right words."

Most of us have known the frustration of a feeling that we could not express. Then someone says it for us. A friend whose boldness we do not mind identifies what is eating away inside us. Someone rises at a public meeting and voices the unarticulated concern that brought us to attend. A tattered paperback going the rounds of the neighborhood proves to be more than a good story. There is a character in it who represents our life, who thinks our thoughts, who shares our dreams, who knows our pain.

Someone understands exactly how we feel. That is what we value. It is the experience of identifying what hidden weight leans against our inner nerve and saps the strength of our deepest self. The right words do not completely remove the load, but they shove it aside. They take away the immediate pressure. We may still be "perplexed" by our inner state, but at least we are "not driven to despair" (II Cor. 4:8).

Prayer is discovering that someone understands us. The psalms make this clear. The psalmists do not sit in a formal drawing room and converse demurely with God over a cup of tea. They do not shuffle into a silent sanctuary and whisper polite requests with pious meekness.

The psalmists have the same feelings we have. The psalmists rage against God. They storm. They plead. They weep. They explode in desperation. They call for vengeance. They exult over their enemies. They are overwhelmed by the grandeur of the universe. They keep silence. They give thanks. They praise God with every instrument in the orchestra.

To read the psalms and to experience them is to know that someone understands exactly how we feel.

Despite the vast cultural differences between the psalmists and us, the fundamental character of people remains. Anger and joy, fear and praise still define the inner state of persons who struggle with life and who seek God's presence.

The earthy, human quality of the psalms has been buried under the church's high-toned liturgical use of them. Of course, the psalms belong in worship. There should be a time for them to sound with dignity and splendor. But ritual is not the only context for the psalms, and reverence is not the only tone in which to read them.

The individual who cries "Deliver me, O Lord, from evil men" (Ps. 140:1) does not speak with placid assurance. Desperate people yell for help, and that is exactly what the psalmist does. His language is not religious. It carries the urgent anguish of a person in panic: "Preserve me from violent men, who have planned to trip up my feet. . . . Let burning coals fall upon them! Let them be cast into pits, no more to rise!" (Ps. 140:4,10).

Because many people are not familiar with the down-to-earth quality of the psalms, they believe that all prayer must be marked by an attitude of reverence and humility. Such a mood is hard to conjure up when we are in the recovery room after surgery or when our child has run away from home or when we have had a bitter argument with the person we love most or when we are exhausted from the day or when we are in the dentist's chair to have an impacted wisdom tooth extracted.

It is a distortion of faith as well as of feeling to think we must assume piety before we can pray. There is no Amy Vanderbilt of etiquette for prayer. Jesus urges us simply to start praying: "Ask, and it will be given you; seek, and you will find; knock, and it will be opened to you" (Matt. 7:7).

Jesus does not even suggest that it is wrong to ask God for something particular, as though that would be too selfish. Jesus realizes that if we hedge prayer in with rules and conventions, most of us will never begin.

A young man once questioned me as to whether it would be all right to pray that a woman he was falling in love with would not move away. The man had never prayed before. He was under the impression that prayer was reserved for weightier matters than romance. I told him to pray for exactly what he wanted. I could not promise that things would work out as he wished, but at least for once in his life the man was striking up a genuine conversation with God.

Getting started is the hardest thing about prayer for many people. The psalms can boost us over this initial obstacle. Provided, that is, we read them as words issuing out of genuine human experience. We need to engage in the psalmists' spontaneous exclamations of feeling and yearning.

To identify with the psalmists is to clarify our own interior state. It is to discover that prayer does not demand pulpit rhetoric and pious jargon. Prayer is much closer to the nerve of daily life. Prayer is the pulse of existence. Its speech is the same language we use when we receive a dozen roses from a friend and when the pain is so bad we ask the doctor for stronger medicine.

A close call with death. The collapse of a nation. The sight of hills. Personal anguish. A thunderstorm. Fed up with the world. Giddy gladness about life. These common experiences are the starting point for many psalms. They can become the starting point for us. A particular feeling or a special experience can be the first word that breaks the silence between God and ourselves. It can be the opener in a conversation that may cover topics we had not thought of discussing and may conclude with decisions we had not planned on making. For prayer does not end where it begins.

Prayer takes us someplace. It moves us beyond ourselves to consider something greater than our immediate situation.

In the psalms the journey from one's private world to the public universe is reflected by a shift in language. The psalmist often opens his prayer in the first person singular but ends up speaking in the third person or imagines himself praising God within the congregation of Israel.

The psalmist whose first words are "Deliver me, O Lord, from evil men" concludes his prayer with a statement of belief:

I know that the Lord maintains the cause of the afflicted,
    and executes justice for the needy.
Surely the righteous shall give thanks to thy name;
    the upright shall dwell in thy presence.

(Ps. 140:12-13)

The psalmist has moved from an anxious plea to an affirmation of trust. The situation that was about to overwhelm him is now manageable. The psalmist can cope. This does not mean that everything has turned out swell or that behind every cloud there is a silver lining or that the psalmist feels completely at peace.

The affirmation of trust in God means that the psalmist's total situation is defined by something greater than what is immediately pressuring him. There is a larger standard for the measurement of existence than one's personal life. The psalmist himself is not experiencing God's vindication. Yet the psalmist knows that this does not cancel the truth of God's justice. Someday, sometime, someplace "the upright shall dwell in thy presence." This belief sustains the psalmist. It lets him endure the terror of the moment by feeding him with the strength of eternity. The psalmist is "persecuted, but not forsaken." He is "struck down, but not destroyed" (II Cor. 4:9).

Through prayer the psalmist has moved from feeling to faith. He has voyaged from the island of himself to the continent of God. It is a difficult and scary trip. Frequently one is tempted to head back to the place from which one embarked. The psalmist seems well on his way toward God—"O Lord, my Lord, my strong deliverer, thou hast covered my head in the day of battle" (Ps. 140:7)—when all of a sudden the violent seas of his immediate problem threaten to swamp the ship: "Those who surround me lift up their head" (Ps. 140:9). But the psalmist persists. He sails through a fresh storm of outward persecution and interior vengeance. Finally, he arrives at his affirmation of faith.

The psalmist's route is our route. We too must voyage from feeling to faith, from experience to truth, from isolation to community, from me to us, from self to God.

The first stage of our journey is not the denial of our private lives. It is the exact opposite. We begin prayer by exploring our personal experience and acknowledging our genuine desires. Jesus includes the request for "daily bread" in his own prayer because if people don't first deal with their grumbling stomachs, it can become a hollow act to claim "Thine is the kingdom and the power and the glory forever."

No fake piety. No bogus humility. No concocted sanctity. "Exactly how I feel" is the starting point of prayer. If I am awed by the majesty of God, then reverence spontaneously fills my being. In the presence of the Lord sacred words are the natural and fitting expression of everything I feel: "Holy, holy, holy is the Lord of hosts; the whole earth is full of his glory" (Isa. 6:3). But if I am angry that my associate has gotten a promotion because he played up to the boss and claimed credit for ideas that were mine, then I shall pray as the psalmist did: "Vindicate me, O God, and defend my cause against an ungodly people; from deceitful and unjust men deliver me!" (Ps. 43:1).

"Exactly how I feel" does not always represent my best side or my most faithful attitude. It is often "exactly how I feel" that cuts me off from accepting a new idea, from forgiving my friend, and from receiving God's grace.

Someone may argue me into a corner in an attempt to convince me that I ought to change an opinion or attitude. But if that person ignores "exactly how I feel," then his finely reasoned eloquence will not change me. All the prayerful words of Scripture cannot move an individual one inch closer to God if they do not clearly relate to that person's interior state.

The power of the psalms is that they do reflect our common life. The psalms connect with our experience. They identify our fundamental humanity, our fears, our hopes, our loves, our hatreds.

The psalmists lose no time searching for an elegant spiritual key to the door of heaven. They grab what is directly at hand. They know that the word of justice and strength which they seek is "not in heaven" and not "beyond the sea" but "very near" (Deut. 30:12ff.). The way to find God is not to abandon earth. Rather, it is to affirm who I am and what I feel. These personal realities are God's secret corridors into the soul. If we stumble toward the distant light that shines at their far end, we will discover that they lead to an open expanse of existence that we would never see if we stayed buried in ourselves.

God has not abandoned us. God has tunneled into our common existence so the Holy Spirit may blow away the stagnant air of self-preoccupation.

We will never find God's passageways if we shut the door to our feelings and look for a more luxuriously spiritual route. The streets within the city of heaven may be "pure gold" (Rev. 21:21), but the roads that lead there are concrete. They have potholes and poorly marked intersections. It is easy to get lost. Fortunately, the psalmists have traveled this way before and they have left the record of their experience.

When people ask us how to get to our home, they want to hear more than "Travel in a northeasterly direction." They want specific directions. Where to turn. Where to exit. What landmarks to look for. It is the little details that keep people from getting lost. The shoe store and the pharmacy on the corner. The dilapidated barn next to the split rail fence where you turn left.

It is the psalmists' sure sense of particulars—looking at a mountain, feeling betrayed, hearing a crash of thunder—that makes their directions so useful. The psalmists are not vaguely spiritual. Their cries are sharp. Their joy is uncontainable. Their requests are clear and direct. We feel the goose bumps of the psalmist who exclaims, "The heavens are telling the glory of God" (Ps. 19:1), and we know the exhaustion of the psalmist who sighs, "I am weary with my crying; my throat is parched. My eyes grow dim with waiting for my God" (Ps. 69:3).

The prayerful directions of the Psalter were not written by a travel agent who has never journeyed from his office. The psalms represent the guidance of people who know the territory through which we must pass.

Because the psalms weld together common life and God's presence, they are a way to understanding the incarnation of Jesus Christ. Through the psalms we glimpse how the ordinary reality of human life could be the perfect expression of God. We experience our own humanity as a contact point between earth and heaven, flesh and spirit. We do not become little incarnations. But we see how someone who was "fully human" might be "fully divine." No longer do we consider "human" and "divine" to be only the mutually exclusive categories of logic. Each is integrally related to the other in the act of prayer. Not the prayer of spooky piety, but the prayer of common life. The prayer that issues spontaneously out of the grit of how we feel.

Jesus Christ. It is to him that the psalmists ultimately move us. Not by calculated argument, but by the genuine experience of finding God through what we touch and feel.

The early church sensed how the psalms disclose the inner dynamics of the incarnation. The psalms reveal how the Spirit can be blended into the substance of human life. That is why the Gospel writers use quotations from the psalms to interpret Christ's life and death. The opening line of Psalm 22, "My God, my God, why hast thou forsaken me?" expresses more than Christ's agony (see Matt. 27:46; Mark 15:34). It stands for the reality of incarnation as experientially depicted in the entire psalm. The psalm shows how one is able to find God's presence by starting from the feeling of abandonment by God.

Jesus' utterance of the psalmist's words points to what incarnation means. It indicates that our common life, even in its most fearful and seemingly godless moments, is where we are to find God. God is present in ordinary things, events, and people. No wonder, then, that God could be fully present in a carpenter from Nazareth.

We begin prayer with exactly how we feel, as Christ did on the cross. We aim to move beyond our immediate interior state to a greater truth. We seek to find in our deepest despair grounds for believing that "all the ends of the earth shall remember and turn to the Lord" (Ps. 22:27). We hope to move from feeling to faith.

2

Close Call

My God, I'm alive! My God, I'm alive! My God, I'm alive!"

We had just missed a head-on collision with a drunk driver. Gordie's uncle had managed to squeeze our car between a road sign and the guardrail. Instead of hitting directly, the cars grated against each other. One second I was enjoying my ride back to college after Thanksgiving. The next second the left side of the car was missing.

I remember stumbling out of the wreck and collapsing on rubber legs and hearing Gordie's aunt repeat: "My God, I'm alive! My God, I'm alive!"

An observer might have dismissed the woman's cry as hysteria, but actually it represented more than a shock reaction. She was praying. There was nothing deliberately religious about her manner, and there was considerable emotional upset. Nevertheless, her cry was prayer. It was addressed to God, and it poured out the one central truth that astounded the woman and filled her with thanks: she was alive.

At the time, I did not recognize the woman's cry as prayer, not even after I gained my own composure. I had always thought of prayer in calmer, more formal terms. The sharp-edged cry of the woman was out of tune with the reverent inflection that I had known in worship and private devotion.

It was not until several years after the accident that I recognized the woman's cry as prayer. A physician said to me, "I have always considered the most genuine prayers to be those spontaneous expressions of pain and hope which I hear from patients in the hospital." I wondered how that could be. I thought prayer had to proceed from conviction and well-reasoned faith. Prayer to me was ritual. Orderly, modest, hushed. Prayer meant a lowered voice, not the pinched, guttural "God!" with which a patient grimaces when an intern has trouble finding a vein for a blood sample. That was not prayer in my book. It was using "God" as an interjection and ignoring the commandment to speak the Lord's name with care (Ex. 20:7).

Daily rounds as a parish pastor have completely reversed my view. I still see the need for reverent prayer, but I have come to appreciate the authenticity of those sighs and pleas which spring from people in distress and from individuals who have escaped death by the skin of their teeth.

A close call leaves us too flabbergasted for eloquence. It fills us with thanks. "My God, I'm alive! My God, I'm alive!" That may be the extent of our language, but brief outbursts of spontaneous joy indicate great depths of gratitude. Genuine thanks are seldom long-winded.

A close call as the occasion of prayer is not foreign to the Bible. It is the harrowing escape from Pharaoh's army which draws forth one of the most ancient responses to God recorded in Scripture: "Sing to the Lord, for he has triumphed gloriously; the horse and his rider he has thrown into the sea" (Ex. 15:21).

It is also a close call that drives the psalmist to exclaim:

> If it had not been the Lord who was on our side,
>   let Israel now say—
> if it had not been the Lord who was on our side,
>   when men rose up against us,
> then they would have swallowed us up alive,
>   when their anger was kindled against us.
>   (Ps. 124:1–3)

These lines have the breathless excitement of someone who has just avoided disaster. We can almost hear the psalmist panting. He starts out with a rush of words, "If it had not been the Lord who was on our side," and next interrupts his thought to include an aside, "Let Israel now say." Then the psalmist begins the story all over, "If it had not been the Lord who was on our side."

The psalmist's speech pattern can be explained as liturgical. The words "Let Israel now say" may be directions for a congregation. However, there is another, more personal way to interpret the psalm.

The psalmist's excitement is familiar to anyone who knows children. A youngster comes home bursting to explain something. He starts his story only to interrupt it with, "You should have been there," and then returns to tell what has happened.

We all are children in the face of a close call. Our reaction rattles the capacity for fluent speech. We have to catch our breath, yet we cannot wait to speak. So we end up, as did the psalmist, starting our story twice.

The psalmist's experience indicates that careful preparation of our inner state is not necessary for every prayer we utter. Prayer can be the spontaneous explosion of relief after a narrow escape.

The psalmist's first word is "if." It is the same key word that people use when they are simply glad to be alive after an accident or to know that someone they love has survived a tight scrape with death. "If my neighbor had not just looked out of the kitchen window. . . ." "If the road did not have a narrow shoulder where I could pull the car over. . . ." "If I had not asked the doctor. . . ." "If the night watchman had not found the tape on the door latch. . . ." "If the dog had not whined at the cellar door. . . ."

The "ifs" of life are the linchpins of existence. Pull them out and life falls to pieces. After a close call, people are frequently so overpowered with the realization of how their whole life depended on a tiny detail that they experience their deliverance as an act of God. The neighbor looking out of the kitchen window and the whining dog are providential. The psalmist captures perfectly what people feel: "The Lord . . . was on our side."

People's experience of providence through the close calls of life is authentic. This experience does not answer the sticky question of why people suffer, but it does provide a positive contact with God's gracious care. When someone escapes tragedy by a hairsbreadth, it is not the occasion to struggle with the complex theological issues of good and evil. It is time to celebrate. To rejoice. To be glad. To tell of deliverance. To pray with breathless wonder to the God who rescues people.

Once the psalmist regains enough composure to speak fluently, he continues his story. He piles up descriptions of the terror that would have overtaken Israel had it not been for God's help:

> then they would have swallowed us up alive,
>   when their anger was kindled against us;
> then the flood would have swept us away,
>   the torrent would have gone over us;
> then over us would have gone the raging waters.
>
> (Ps. 124:3–5)

The language is clearly influenced by Israel's most central experience: the escape from Egypt and the miraculous deliverance at the Red Sea. But more is at work in the psalmist's speech than the exodus.

The psalmist is using language that is rooted in the pit of our fear and in the fiber of our anxiety. "Swallowed us up alive," "The flood would have swept us away," "Over us would have gone the raging waters"—this is visceral speech. It is the way a shaken person talks. It is not playing around with religious metaphors. People speak like this when they have felt the bottom of their stomach drop away.

Prayer does not always use placid or exalted language. The words for prayer in an emergency come from the center of feeling. Prayer is not pretty poetry. Prayer is accurate expression. Prayer is our weak knees and our hollow innards as we cry: "My God, I'm alive! My God, I'm alive!"

The psalmist has not yet addressed a single word directly to God. This is significant. It indicates the possibility of starting prayer without immediately speaking to God. Many people do this. They reflect on their experience. They consider the terrifying things that might have happened to them. This inner process can become prayer as people turn from a conversation with themselves to including God more directly. The psalmist does this:

> Blessed be the Lord,
> Who has not given us
> as prey to their teeth!
> (Ps. 124:6)

The psalmist does not go into a long song and dance about God. He keeps it short and to the point: "Blessed be the Lord."

Clearly the psalmist remains more wrapped up in the escape than anything else. Praising God leads into new reflections on the terror of what might have happened.

> We have escaped as a bird
> from the snare of the fowlers;
> the snare is broken,
> and we have escaped!
> (Ps. 124:7)

This is terrifying language. To be a bird that hunters are trying to trap. That is how we feel when it looks as though the giant pincers of history or the hand of death is about to crush us. We are frightened animals at the mercy of forces we do not comprehend. Life is vulnerable. Therefore it is understandable to God that our first response to a close call will be endless fascination that we escaped. Whatever direct praise we offer will be brief. "Blessed be the Lord" is about all we can say until we get the fright out of our system.

People recovering from accidents often relive their experience over and over. Like the psalmist they keep reflecting on what might have been. Not until they have repeatedly considered the event are they ready to pray more dispassionately.

> Our help is in the name of the Lord,
> who made heaven and earth.
> (Ps. 124:8)

These are the psalmist's final words. They are grand, reassuring words. Words of faith. Words that leave far behind the panic of a close call. Words that bring us into the majesty and glory of God.

It turns out that we were not simply at the mercy of hostile forces. We were not the "prey" of cruel hunters. There was someone else in control all the time while we and the psalmist were shaking in our shoes. This world is more than "a darkling plain / Swept with confused alarms of struggle and flight, / Where ignorant armies clash by night" (Matthew Arnold, "Dover Beach"). This world is the creation of God. God is here. Present. Alive. Active.

We and the psalmist make our affirmation on more than blind faith and more than a happy life. We have had a close call with death. We have faced the terror of our experience head on. We have not hidden it underneath pious phrases, but have called a spade a spade. We were nearly swallowed, drowned, captured, and eaten. It was terrifying. Life can be terrifying. We understand why people think this world to be "a darkling plain." We have felt the same way ourselves.

But when we struggled through our panic, when we escaped by the skin of our teeth, we were touched by something. Some power. Some presence. Some gracious strength that was greater than the horror that surrounded us. We discovered that no matter what terrors the world held for us, we were still held in God's hand.

We and the psalmist did not find this in a peaceful, reflective religious moment. We found it in strenuous prayer. Prayer wrung out of a close call. God was present in the most seemingly godless time.

The church has isolated the psalmist's affirmation of faith from the psalmist's experience of the world. As a regular member of the Presbyterian church, I had frequently heard these words as a call to worship: "Our help is in the name of the Lord, who made heaven and earth." It was not until seminary that I hooked them up with the psalmist's excruciating experience.

The church has good grounds for choosing the psalmist's final verse as a liturgical formula. It is a magnificent expression of why the church gathers to worship. Still, the contrast between hearing the final words as an isolated unit and hearing them as issuing out of experience is revealing. It symbolizes the potential distortions of a faith that is not grounded in the common experience of people. Such a faith gives the impression that the greatest affirmations of God's power are shot down from heaven in hermetically sealed tubes. When in fact the pronouncements of heaven penetrate earth through the pores of common experience.

A close call. Not heavenly angels. Not ecstatic visions. Not inspiring worship. But a narrow escape from death. Something that leaves us with sweaty palms and a need to sit down before we fall down from fright. In that shaky moment of astonishment and relief lies the substance of a true prayer. Perhaps all it will start with is "My God, I'm alive! My God, I'm alive!" But once our initial shock dissipates, then we may pray with overwhelming conviction: "Our help is in the name of the Lord, who made heaven and earth."

3

The Tree
and the Dandelion

Every morning the woman talked to her tree. After breakfast and the *Today Show* she would take a second cup of coffee, sit on the sun porch, and converse with the maple tree in her backyard.

Thirty-eight years ago, when she first moved in, the woman had planted that tree. Her brother had given it to her. "Maple trees are hardy," he said, and he was right. The elms out front had been removed some years ago, and the clump of birches had yellow, mangy leaves. But the maple was still straight and strong and full.

The woman remembered a May snowstorm that dumped four inches of heavy, soggy snow on the young sapling. The leaves were already out, so the branches accumulated a massive load of white glop. The woman had dashed out during the night in her slippers and housecoat to knock the snow off the tree with the kitchen broom.

Then there was the time the children had moved the swing too far out on a branch. When they all climbed on the swing together, there was a snapping, splintering sound, and the woman had to call a tree surgeon. For a while the tree had the asymmetrical appearance of a boy who had given himself a haircut with shears from the sewing basket.

But all of this was years ago. Now one could not even tell where the branch had been sawed off. The tree had survived the antics of children and the temper tantrums of nature. It was shade in the summer and fire in the autumn, a guardian in the winter and a debutante in a diaphanous green gown in the spring.

The woman delighted in the tree's seasonal changes. They were a dependable standard by which she marked and cataloged the flow of her own life. She would look at the tree and remember what she had been doing last year when the buds were out to the same point. Next she would reflect on each successive spring until it became difficult to distinguish one year from another. The only thing clear in her mind was that the tree had witnessed the living of her life. Then the woman wondered if she had grown to be as rooted and strong and dependable as the tree.

When the woman said she "talked" to her tree this is what she meant: not that she had a conversation with the tree, but that the tree initiated an inner dialogue. The tree's physical features—its roots, its trunk, its branches, its seasonal changes—roused the woman to search for interior affinities that would make her as secure about herself as she was about the growth and strength of her beloved maple. The woman wanted to be like her tree. In this desire she was similar to the psalmist who writes that the righteous person

> is like a tree
> planted by streams of water,
> that yields its fruit in its season,
> and its leaf does not wither.
> In all that he does, he prospers.
> (Ps. 1:3)

Prayer is sinking roots into the soil of God's word and being watered by God's Spirit.

Prayer is intuiting the interior reality of our life through the exterior world. The woman and the psalmist understood their relationship to God through their encounter with a tree. They knew what a tree is, not in terms of genus and species, but in terms of its character and meaning. The tree "spoke" to them. It addressed them in the same way that a painting or a poem does.

The tree gave shape to their previously amorphous yearnings. It was like the particle which a chemist drops into a solution in order to crystallize out a particular substance. The tree crystallized certain fundamental choices that the woman and the psalmist had to make: In what will my life be rooted? What will my life produce? How will I sustain the droughts and the storms of being human?

Prayer is looking at a tree and being personally confronted with these choices.

The woman knew she wanted deep roots. That is why she had moved to the neighborhood in the first place. Thirty-eight years ago the area had marked the far edge of the city. There was even a dairy farm down the street. But the farm had been sold and subdivided into lots following World War II. The last vestige of rural life had disappeared twenty years ago as tracts of ranch style houses, convenient food marts, and shopping centers took over. For the woman, her maple tree was the sole reminder of the countryside that had been bulldozed under the earth and sealed shut with asphalt.

The tree established in the woman's mind a sense of home, a feeling that in the midst of her shifting world there was at least one symbol of strength and faithfulness. These were the same qualities which the woman wanted at the center of her life. When she sat looking at the tree with her cup of coffee, she was filled with the desire to root her existence in God.

Prayer is allowing the moisture of God's Spirit and the nutrients of God's word to penetrate the buried fibers of our inner selves. Prayer is extending the roots of our being into the ground of existence.

The psalmist instructs us in how to nurture this process:

> Blessed is the man
>   who walks not in the counsel of the wicked,
> nor stands in the way of sinners,
>   nor sits in the seat of the scoffers;
> but his delight is in the law of the Lord,
>   and on his law he meditates day and night.
>   (Ps. 1:1–2)

We could easily misuse these verses to sanction a holier-than-thou attitude and to justify our not associating with people we deem morally unfit. If we did this, we would not only be denying Christ, who sought out the company of sinners, but we would also be distorting the psalmist's most important message.

The psalm lays before us two fundamental patterns by which we can shape our lives: either "the counsel of the wicked" (v. 1) or "the law of the Lord" (v. 2).

The word "counsel" refers to practical instruction or guidance. *The New English Bible* captures this meaning by translating the psalm's first line: "Happy is the man who does not take the wicked for his guide."

Prayer is deciding who will guide our lives. Prayer is choosing the model of existence that will structure who we are and what we do.

If we choose "the law of the Lord," that does not mean the matter is over and done with. The psalmist talks about how one "meditates day and night" on the law.

Day and night!

Does this mean that prayer entails becoming a religious recluse who focuses exclusively on the pursuit of piety? No, it does not, as becomes clear when we understand the words "law" and "meditate."

God tells Joshua to "meditate on [the law] day and night" (Josh. 1:8). But God binds this instruction to promises of leading the people into Canaan. Only three verses after the command to "meditate," Joshua is busy organizing the people to pass over the Jordan. Clearly, meditation in the Bible is not synonymous with inactivity. While building a new nation, the people are to hold before them the ways of God.

Meditation does not preclude the strenuous efforts of creating a government and a culture. Meditation allows God's justice and integrity to flow through the interior lives of people into their social and political activism.

The psalmist's meditation is not a dreamy mindlessness. It has a particular focus: "the law of the Lord."

"Law" means God's teaching or instruction. It includes God's actions in history as well as God's commandments.

Meditation, for the psalmist, does not center on the individual's state of consciousness. Rather, it involves concentrating on what God has revealed in the world of human events. The interior act of meditation is aimed at the exterior manifestations of God.

Private prayer connects an individual to the God of history.

Prayer is using one's personal inner life to grasp the power that moves within yet stands beyond the upheavals of the world. Prayer anchors people in God so that the storms of history do not blow them away.

I once knew a Czechoslovakian woman who had gone through hell in her native country. War, hunger, and disease had taken a number of family and friends. She had escaped. A devout person, she used to go into a church every day to pray, because, as she said, "It keeps me standing."

> The wicked are not so,
>   but are like chaff which the wind drives away.
> Therefore the wicked will not stand in
>   the judgment,
>   nor sinners in the congregation of the
>   righteous.
>
> (Ps. 1:4–5)

The psalmist describes here the alternative to grounding one's life in God. It is to become like the useless siftings of wheat which are carried away by the wind in the process of threshing grain.

The psalmist overstates his case. The facts of life are: the wicked prosper and the righteous perish. Anyone who reads the newspaper or lives in the workaday world knows that.

Before we dismiss the psalmist as a pietistic Pollyanna, however, we must realize that he is describing more than the world of human relationships. He is probing beneath the injustices of common life to that level of existence at which an individual stands before God. The entire foundation of the psalmist's claim is not belief in human fairness but faith in divine justice:

> for the Lord knows the way of the righteous,
>   but the way of the wicked will perish.
>
> (Ps. 1:6)

The Lord's knowledge of us is more than a casual acquaintance with the outline of our lives. It is intimacy with our essential character. If we were to write down every thought, every feeling, every action, and every experience of our lives, the sum total of our data would not equal God's knowledge of us. "Such knowledge is too wonderful for [us]; it is high, [we] cannot attain it" (Ps. 139:6).

God has such knowledge. And because God knows us this thoroughly, the psalmist proclaims that the righteous "prosper," while "the way of the wicked will perish."

Note the last word: perish. It is a common word in the Old Testament and one that we would like to forget.

Moses warns the Israelites that if they follow other gods, they shall "perish" (Deut. 30:18). Not be given a hundred-dollar fine and a thirty-day suspended sentence, but perish! Vanish. Be annihilated. Exist no longer. It is on this terrifying thought that the psalmist ends.

We must not seek to blunt the psalm's sharp edge with God's mercy. There are other Biblical passages that provide mercy in abundance, but the power of this psalm is its judgment, and it is a judgment that we require. For if prayer brings only mercy, our relationship to God will be halfhearted and sentimental.

In prayer God's judgment moves us beyond a wishy-washy faith. We are confronted with a clear choice: the way of the righteous or the way of the wicked. We must choose one. We cannot have a little of each. Either we are a tree or we are chaff.

Perhaps "chaff" is an antiquated image for a society that pours its breakfast cereal out of a box and buys its bread in double plastic bags. If so, we might replace chaff with a more common scene: dandelions gone to seed.

Prayer is what keeps faith from becoming like the feathery fluff of the weed which is scattered by the breeze. Prayer is reaching into God so that we no longer are "tossed to and fro and carried about with every wind of doctrine" (Eph. 4:14). We do not buy into every fad; we are not swept away by every new movement; we do not become a part of every hot cause.

We stand in the midst of the world, and we relate to the world. But there is a steady strength to our posture, a faithfulness about our actions and our speech. It is prayer that gives us this character. Prayer is becoming a tree whose roots extend into the depths of God.

4

Forgiven

The digital clock radio flipped the number on the right. 12:47. The silence of the night streets made my friend's voice seem louder than it was. There were no passing cars or people on the sidewalks to fill in the gaps between his weeping and his speaking. His wife had run away about eight hours ago.

"Things have not been too good between her and me for some time now. I know that I've done a lot wrong, a lot of terrible things. But I thought we might forgive each other. I've prayed and prayed that she would forgive me and I her, that we would quit keeping track of our failures, and we'd start again. But it's never worked."

The guilt and the night and the yearning for forgiveness reminded me of the psalmist. He too was waiting in the dark for the first glimmer of forgiveness. "My soul waits for the Lord more than watchmen for the morning, more than watchmen for the morning" (Ps. 130:6).

Forgiveness. From childhood on we hear a lot of words about it. Parents tell youngsters: "Now shake hands and make up. You must forgive each other." When we are a little older, perhaps we pick up the cliché, "To err is human, to forgive, divine." And in many churches Sunday after Sunday the pastor announces a declaration of pardon: "In the name of Jesus Christ you are forgiven."

Despite all the words, forgiveness eludes us. Sometimes we forgive another person. We are helped in this by our sense of control over the situation. It is we who are being gracious, and that is a good feeling. We like the magnanimous role of saying "I forgive you."

But to accept forgiveness is altogether more difficult. It is hard to leave behind the wrong which haunts us. Every time we try to step out of the past into the future we cut our conscience on the fragments of our shattered integrity. We cannot sweep our inner selves clean of regret and self-accusation. "Why did I do that? It's not like me. What has gotten into me? My God, I really sold out on everything I stand for. I'll never live with myself again." Sin's stain is most permanent when it smudges the white of our own soul. It takes something more powerful to cleanse our guilt than the repeated assurance of pardon from the one whom we wronged.

We are paralyzed by guilt. Like the man lowered through the roof on his cot (Mark 2:2ff.), we cannot walk, because we are immobilized by our sense of having done wrong.

Some modern persons might dismiss guilt as the pathological holdover of a less sophisticated age. There is no longer need for people to burden themselves with a sense of sin. We all slip up sometimes, but that is to be expected. After all, "everybody does it."

The contemporary strategy for avoiding the pain of guilt is not new. It's been tried before. "The fool says in his heart, 'There is no God.' They are corrupt, they do abominable deeds, there is none that does good" (Ps. 14:1).

The strategy frequently falters in the face of personal upheaval. 12:47 A.M. A man's wife has run away and the log jam of past wrongs that was building up in the tributaries of the mind breaks and flows into the mainstream of consciousness. The couple's initial and very contemporary intention of "never feeling guilt about each other" is seen for what it really is: an illusion. "If we say we have no sin, we deceive ourselves, and the truth is not in us" (I John 1:8).

The psalmist knows how painful it is to give up the deception of innocence:

> Out of the depths I cry to thee, O Lord!
>   Lord, hear my voice!
> Let thy ears be attentive
>   to the voice of my supplications!
>
> (Ps. 130:1–2)

Turning to God to relieve our guilt is not easy. It involves crying from our "depths." We would rather speak from our shallows. We are eager to tell God of our superficial wrongs. The angry word, the tidbit of gossip, the latest private indulgence, the scheming daydream, the thoughtless remark. If we quickly unload these, then we can snatch God's grace and get on with living. Our guilt will be done with, and we'll feel, oh, so good inside.

Confession is more than wiping away life's little wrongs with the once-over of a hasty prayer: "I'm sorry, God." Confession is crying from the depths. It is probing my fundamental character as a human being and discovering that the core of my personal existence is out of alignment with the truth.

My noblest thoughts and actions do not come across as I had hoped. They are always distorted by the limits of my perception, by the inadequacy of my knowledge, by the power of hidden self-interest, and by forces of the external world. I accrue to my life's account more wrongs than my credit entitles me. I am aware, along with the psalmist, that "if thou, O Lord, shouldst mark iniquities, Lord, who could stand?" (Ps. 130:3).

But I *am* still standing! Still living. Still making my way through life's daily rounds. Prayer confronts me with this fact. I knew it all along, but I was never so amazingly aware of it until I prayed. Despite my sin, I can still operate in the world. God has not struck me down. God has not given up on me. The very act of calling to God, combined with my continuing existence, leads me to see: "But there is forgiveness with thee, that thou mayest be feared" (Ps. 130:4).

My pardon is a function of something greater than self-acceptance and the generosity of other people. Forgiveness rests on nothing so fleeting as a comfortable conscience or the approval of my peers.

In God I discover a standard of judgment and a power for forgiveness that are independent of humanity.

God judges. God forgives.

Because of this objective, transcendent reality, the pressure of my own guilt is eased. At any one moment I may feel the terrible burden of my wrong. Yet never does it crush me. Always I am aware that "there is forgiveness with thee."

Prayer is renewing the sense of God's forgiveness. It is heightening my interior awareness of divine pardon. It is letting God lift the coffin lid of guilt so I can breathe again.

I facilitate God's lifting action by ceasing to consider human opinion a realistic judge of my essential being. Paul explains the process clearly: "But with me it is a very small thing that I should be judged by you or by any human court. I do not even judge myself. I am not aware of anything against myself, but I am not thereby acquitted. It is the Lord who judges me" (I Cor. 4:3–4).

We may feel guilty or we may feel innocent, but guilt and innocence are ultimately judgments that only God can make. Our forgiveness does not depend on the unpredictable compassion of a human jury. We are at the mercy of the Lord, who is "slow to anger and abounding in steadfast love" (Ps. 103:8).

Belief in God's mercy does not bring instant relief. It frequently takes time for the affirmations of faith to seep into the bloodstream and to penetrate the heart. "I believe; help my unbelief!" (Mark 9:24) is a motto for all people who trust in God's mercy but still find themselves mired in guilt. There is often a period of waiting between the declaration of pardon and the feeling of personal acceptance. Thus, the psalmist who affirms God's forgiveness continues to pray:

> I wait for the Lord, my soul waits,
>   and in his word I hope;
> my soul waits for the Lord
>   more than watchmen for the morning,
>   more than watchmen for the morning.
>   (Ps. 130:5–6)

Prayer is waiting for the truth of God's mercy to become the personal truth of our life.

Waiting is not passive, but active. The Hebrew word for "wait" may refer to stretching and twisting together the strands of a rope. Prayer is twisting into one cord our belief and our feeling. It is entwining our lives with God's mercy until we have a rope of faith strong enough to tug us out of the depths of guilt.

We cannot manufacture the rope on a machine. There are no

easy formulas or special words that will make us feel forgiven. Prayer is not an automated process for the production of personal faith.

Prayer weaves faith by hand. It takes Scripture, worship, conversation, feeling, thought, and experience and tries to braid them together. Prayer is figuring out in the presence of God what God has to do with me. I struggle with God to discover how God's forgiveness is real for me.

Prayer takes time. It can be very discouraging. We may grow more impatient for God's forgiveness than the ancient watchmen were for the morning light.

We would stop praying except that God prays with us. The Spirit breathes in our imperfect human words.

Although prayer pulls together many strands from our common life, it also works with the unbreakable fiber of God's grace. Therefore we do not give up. We know that our efforts are reinforced by a strength greater than our own.

Prayer is discovering the total reliability of God's forgiveness. Prayer is realizing that we can start again. The past no longer dictates the future. The "depths" of guilt do not limit the heights of hope. Christ's words to the adulteress are addressed directly to each of us: "Neither do I condemn you; go, and do not sin again" (John 8:11).

Not condemned! We shudder in amazement. God is "feared" (Ps. 130:4) because God forgives. Not a scary fear, but an awesome fear.

God's love "casts out" the scary fear (I John 4:18). But it awakens an entirely different kind of fear. It is a combination of awe and mystery and astonishment. How can God be this loving? It is a fearful wonder to our uncomprehending flesh. It leaves us with the same weakness we feel when the "Hallelujah Chorus" makes every hair stand on end. It is like the anxious tremble of the young couple who behold their first child. How could life this precious and fragile come from us?

Prayer is fearful. It starts us shaking with incredulous belief. We believe what seems too wonderful to believe: that we who were estranged from God have been reconciled to God. What kind of God is this whose forgiveness is deeper than the depths of our guilt?

A God to be feared, a God to be held in awe and reverence and honor.

Our liberation from guilt reshapes our relationship to others. Because we have been forgiven, we become forgiving. Because we have been accepted, we become accepting. Because we have been set free, we announce this freedom to others:

> O Israel, hope in the Lord!
>   For with the Lord there is steadfast love,
>   and with him is plenteous redemption.
> And he will redeem Israel
>   from all his iniquities.

(Ps. 130:7–8)

Hope in the Lord. What does that mean? We hope for so many things in life. We hope it will be a nice day for the picnic. We hope our son or daughter will make it home for Thanksgiving. We hope for a speedy recovery from the operation. We hope our candidate will win the election. We hope a runaway wife will return. We hope we'll receive a raise. We hope our child will soon get over a pouting, moody stage. We hope for world peace.

Is hope in the Lord just one more hope next to all the others we have? No. Hope in the Lord is trusting that behind the universe lies a friendly power who will someday conquer every evil and destructive force. This trust facilitates a hopeful attitude about the events of common life. But this trust does not depend on the fulfillment of our finite hopes. Quite to the contrary. We endure the frustration of our human hopes because we draw strength from our more fundamental reliance on God. If every hope of success and health is crushed, there is still one hope that will not let us down. There is a resilience to life whose tensile strength will never snap. Hoping in the Lord is hanging on to that strength.

Prayer is sorting through our vast collection of human hopes and realizing that something is missing. It is not that our hopes are wicked or unworthy. They simply lack something. All of them taken together cannot speak to the "depths" of being a person and being estranged from the source of existence. Prayer is facing up to the inadequacy of our everyday hopes. It is crying out of the depths and finding a hope that keeps life from overwhelming us.

In prayer we discover that the world is not as poverty-stricken for love as it appears to be. There is a treasury of love and mercy that will never go bankrupt. Its capital is not the fleeting currency of human passion and sentimental affection. Its reserves are backed by something more reliable than the gold standard: "For with the Lord there is steadfast love, and with him is plenteous redemption."

"Redemption" is not a fancy religious word for the psalmist. In a period of history when slavery was common, "redemption" was a word out of everyday life. It is only our distance in time and culture that has made it sound strangely theological. Redemption is being set free.

Our interior "redemption" from guilt is as real as Israel's escape from Egypt, as real as an ancient slave's being freed from his master. Still we comprehend political and legal reality more vividly than the inner motions of the soul. Outer redemption is visual. We can point to a particular historical act. There is a simplicity and directness about it that we can describe.

Deuteronomy captures the lively graphic quality of political redemption. It records words of instruction that an ancient Israelite was to share with his son: "We were Pharaoh's slaves in Egypt; and the Lord brought us out of Egypt with a mighty hand; and the Lord showed signs and wonders, great and grievous, against Egypt and against Pharaoh and all his household, before our eyes" (Deut. 6:21–22). If only the inside of people could be described as clearly as this! Then "redemption from sin" would not sound like some vague preacher's phrase.

Prayer is the process that makes redemption from sin as vivid as cutting iron manacles from a slave's wrists. Prayer does this by taking guilt seriously. Prayer recognizes that guilt's weight and pressure are as real as the demands of an oppressive government. Genuine prayer does not skip merrily along to forgiveness without first realizing how tightly bound we are to our sense of wrong.

Prayer does not depend on human resources for cutting the chains of guilt. Prayer looks to the same power that has freed people from political oppression to free the inner self. This is the significance of the psalmist's turning from "I" to "Israel" in the final verses. The change symbolizes an identification with the history of Israel.

Guilt is no longer solely egocentric. My guilt is part of a greater reality, the pervasiveness of sin. I realize that my personal estrangement is only a particular manifestation of a greater human predicament: "All have sinned and fall short of the glory of God" (Rom. 3:23).

Recognizing the larger dimensions of my dilemma invalidates searching for a purely personal and psychological resolution. Something greater is needed than feeling good about myself again. That would only speak to my immediate subjective state. And there is no telling when good feelings will slide back into bad feelings.

Something more universal is required. I need a power for redemption that realigns not just me but all people with the truth behind the universe.

Prayer is the foundry of the soul where I find my private desire for pardon melted and forged into one piece with humanity's need for forgiveness. My cry from the depths is the cry of all people in the presence of God.

The awareness of universal sin keeps me from becoming buried in myself. I probe the depths of my guilt, but I do not become lost in the maze of self-accusation and self-flagellation. Neither do I dismiss my sin as the illusion of a distraught self. I know that sin is part of being human. The evidence for it is too strong to deny.

Prayer deals with sin in the light of how God has redeemed people in the past. The exodus. The covenant. The prophets. Jesus Christ. Prayer makes these into more than historical events. The Biblical stories become accounts of how God relates to me. This does not happen automatically. I immerse myself in the stories. I explore their personal ramifications by identifying patterns of existence which my life shares with the ancient servants of God. The particular wrong that drove the psalmist to cry from the depths may not be the same as mine, but the reality of guilt remains. The manifestation of redemption may be different now than in ancient times, but the truth of liberation remains.

Prayer is discerning in my life the unchanging patterns of God's grace that are revealed in the Bible. Prayer makes redemption an interior act of liberation. It is as real to me as the escape from Egypt was for an ancient Israelite. I experience redemption as surely as I feel release from pain through the surgeon's skillful knife. Biblically honed prayer excises guilt.

"Redemption" is more than a religious word. It is the concrete experience of being set free in a uniquely personal way. "Redemption" means I am free to argue with my wife again and not worry that she will bring up past wrongs. "Redemption" means I am free to challenge my boss without fear of losing my job because of former failures. "Redemption" means I am free to debate politics with someone of another race and not feel that every disagreement is a sign of bigotry. "Redemption" means I am free to work on the world food crisis without feeling guilty that I still enjoy eating.

All the little acts of redemption point to a greater liberation. They flow from God's power for forgiveness. They remind me that with God "is plenteous redemption." Not miserly, but "plenteous." Abundant forgiveness. Forgiveness so great that it utterly eradicates every trace of guilt. Forgiveness so broad that it "will redeem Israel from *all* his iniquities" (Ps. 130:8; italics added).

God is not picayunish about what will be forgiven and what will be held against us. God does not say we can go free on some counts but must take the rap on others. When we call from the depths, when we "confess our sins," then we find that God "is faithful and just, and will forgive our sins and cleanse us from all unrighteousness" (I John 1:9).

To confess sins is more than the ritual act of reading a unison prayer with the congregation. It is to acknowledge the most excruciating truth of my life. I am not what I ought to be. In the very act of admitting this I find redemption. I am freed from the need to keep up a false front about myself. I no longer carry on the charade of perfectionism. It is replaced with a simpler ceremony that lays aside the pompous costume of self-righteousness and wears the modest garment of faltering humanity.

"Out of the depths I cry to thee, O Lord!" I cry and then I wait. A long wait. A stretched-out period of time that fills me with more impatience than the watchmen of the night who crane their necks toward the east for dawn's first meager evidence. Yet at last the answer: "With the Lord there is steadfast love, and with him is plenteous redemption."

5

Laughter

On the other side of the one-way mirror was a small room. It had a plain table with two chairs. Psychiatrists, nurses, social workers, and chaplains gathered in front of the mirror to observe the state hospital's weekly case study.

A patient and an interviewer entered the small room. The patient was a tall, heavy-boned man. He sat down with such energy that it appeared he would drive the chair through the floor.

The interviewer asked the patient to recount why he had first come to the hospital. The man responded that the police had picked him up for stapling campaign posters to every tree, bench, telephone pole, and parking meter he could find in a one-block area. The place looked as though it had been wallpapered with political advertisements.

"Why did you do this?" asked the interviewer.

"Because I was paid by the candidates."

"But your admission report says that you put up posters for every party and office seeker even though they were running against each other."

"That's true; I did. But they were all willing to pay me, and besides, it doesn't matter who gets in anyway."

The staff laughed. It was the laughter of recognition. There was truth in what the patient said, and his bold statement took the focus off himself and placed it on the world of politics.

After the interview and after the staff had discussed the patient's problem of hyper-energy, the informal chatter returned to the man's remark, "It doesn't matter who gets in anyway." Again the staff laughed. They discussed the coming election and joked about the candidates and their promises. Usually when the staff talked politics, their voices had a tense, earnest tone that was on the verge of breaking into anger. This time their conversation was playful and relaxed.

The patient had freed the staff to smile at politics. He had brought them closer to God's perception of the world's power struggles:

> He who sits in the heavens laughs;
> the Lord has them in derision.
> (Ps. 2:4)

God laughs at politics. Wheeling and dealing, smoke-filled rooms, press releases, power plays, creating a public image—God sees them all for what they really are. But God, unlike people, does not get sucked into taking the whole business too seriously. We know from our private lives that laughter brings objectivity. To laugh at ourselves is often the first step in untangling a difficult problem. This personal insight reflects a societal truth: Laughter strips away the pretentiousness of politics. Laughter frees us from considering something to be holy that is in fact nothing more than human invention and expediency.

The comic quality of the world's power struggles is not apparent to people so long as their perspective is exclusively political. If human beings and their institutions constitute the only force that shapes world events, then politics represents the highest power to which people can appeal for the establishment of justice. Politics becomes sacred.

Such people do not dare to laugh. They throw themselves into the political process with a frantic, blinding fervor. Their cause becomes their God.

This is what happened to Israel's neighbors. They were hell-bent on Israel's destruction. The psalmist pictures them as completely absorbed in their own political schemes and as utterly oblivious to God's deeper plans:

> Why do the nations conspire,
> and the peoples plot in vain?
> The kings of the earth set themselves,
> and the rulers take counsel together,

against the Lord and his anointed, saying,
"Let us burst their bonds asunder,
    and cast their cords from us."

                                        (Ps. 2:1–3)

The nations and rulers are not aware of the absurdity of their actions. Their only basis for judging themselves is their own "counsel" (v. 2).

The psalmist, however, has a different vantage point from which to view events. He heard God laughing at the nations. This reminds him that the world's rulers are not the ultimate power behind history. The political situation does not overwhelm the psalmist. He has an objectivity which enables him to question "why" (v. 1) the nations even bother to concoct their schemes and to form their alliances.

Prayer is looking objectively at politics. It is reading the daily paper or turning on the news and seeing the absurdity of human efforts that are at odds with God's will. Prayer is laughing with God at the world!

To join in heaven's laughter is not to give up on politics. It is not to become haughty and think that politics is too messy for any one of sound character and high ideals. Genuine prayer does not lead to political unconcern. Rather, prayer clarifies the direction of politics by comparing the immediate struggles of the world with God's goal for history.

First we hear God's laughter—we see the absurdity and pretentiousness of politics. Then we feel God's judgment.

The judgment is always there, but we cannot perceive it if we take politics too seriously. Laughter tears away the cloak of seriousness. Our corrupt and empty politics stand exposed to the judgment of God:

Then he will speak to them in his wrath,
    and terrify them in his fury, saying,
"I have set my king
    on Zion, my holy hill."
I will tell of the decree of the Lord:
He said to me, "You are my son,

> today I have begotten you.
> Ask of me, and I will make the nations
>   your heritage,
> and the ends of the earth your possession.
> You shall break them with a rod of iron,
>   and dash them in pieces like a potter's
>   vessel."
>
> (Ps. 2:5–9)

The psalmist does not rise completely above his own political bias. He pictures God as on the side of Israel's king. The psalm may have been used during an enthronement ceremony, with the king possibly speaking vs. 7–9.

Jesus Christ reveals the profounder and more universal meaning of the psalm. Christ is the son who is "begotten" (v. 7) of God (see Acts 13:33). Christ shall judge the politics of every nation and every ruler and every people.

It is not true that there is no standard of conduct for public office. It is not true that a politician can get away with anything and never fear punishment. It is not true that whoever has the most money will always be in power. "Politics as usual" will not be the politics of eternity. Christ's justice leaves no room for shady deals and cover-ups, for laundered funds and self-interest groups, for favoritism and prejudice, for militarism and oppression.

Prayer is tasting Christ's final judgment now. Prayer is being devastated by the infinite distance between the equality we proclaim and the injustice we practice.

We hear something shatter inside ourselves. It is our precious collection of slogans and clichés and excuses. They have turned out to be more fragile than chinaware. Christ has broken them "with a rod of iron" and "dash[ed] them in pieces like a potter's vessel." Our theological vision removes our ideological blindness.

Christ's judgment brings political wisdom. We do not despair. We are called to repent:

> Now therefore, O kings, be wise;
>   be warned, O rulers of the earth.
> Serve the Lord with fear,
>   with trembling kiss his feet,

> lest he be angry, and you perish in the way;
> for his wrath is quickly kindled.
>
> Blessed are all who take refuge in him.
> (Ps. 2:10–12)

The state does not command the highest allegiance. There is a greater power to be served: the Lord.

Subservience to God transcends national distinction and political division. The psalmist does not single out a particular leader. It is the "rulers of the earth" who are to acknowledge God.

"Blessed are *all* who take refuge in God." Prayer obliterates the distinctions of friend and enemy, of this nation against that nation. In prayer we discover that the supreme political value is obedience to the power who rules history.

Prayer does not reveal how we are to act on every issue. Prayer does not take our obedience to God and turn us into the political lackeys of heaven, as though God's will could be reduced to a party line!

Rather, prayer makes us political realists. By keeping us in touch with God's transcendent purpose, prayer enables us to see the world of human affairs as it actually is. We laugh about its absurdities. We replace our illusions of building utopia with a conviction that God shall one day bring justice. This conviction does not result in political apathy, but renews our struggle for a just society. We seek to align our public existence with God's ultimate purpose as revealed in Scripture and confirmed in prayer. Participation in social causes is an expression of prayerful faith.

First comes laughter.

Then judgment.

Next repentance.

And finally renewed engagement with the world.

This is the pattern of prayer when we are alive to both the politics of earth and the rule of God.

6

At the Sight of Hills

Mountains cut us down to size. They remind us how tiny and insignificant we are, how the earth was here long before we were and how it will be here long after we are gone. Mountains have the permanence that we yearn to possess but shall never achieve ourselves. They compel us to face how fleeting human existence is and to ask: What truth shall be the foundation of my life?

When we climb mountains, when we ski, when we travel to the national parks, when we gaze at the hills about our home, then we feel the vastness of the world and the smallness of humanity. We sense in a modern way the ancient intuition that a mountaintop brings us close to God. We understand the psalmist who exclaims:

> I lift up my eyes to the hills.
> From whence does my help come?
> (Ps. 121:1)

A fearful pause follows the psalmist's question. The pause is not indicated by the text, but it is there in the mind. We know this because we join the psalmist in asking the same thing. The hills leave us awestruck, and we too ponder: "From whence does my help come?" We cannot give the lightning response of a TV quiz show participant. We seek more than information. The answer is not a simple matter such as giving the date of the Spanish Armada or recalling who starred in the original screen version of *Pride and Prejudice*. We are not after cold facts. We do not want some scientific or statistical answer whose correctness we can check in *The World Almanac*.

Our question is reflective. It is stimulated by the sight of hills, but it rises to the mind out of the marrow of our bones and the beating of our hearts and the breathing of our lungs. The sight of enduring physical reality sharpens the experience of organic life.

During the fearful pause we are tempted to answer the question prematurely: "From the hills comes my help." For the psalmist this would have been a doubly meaningful answer, since hills were frequently the location of a sanctuary as well as a geological feature of the land.

We may no longer build our sanctuaries on mountaintops, but we are still tempted to find our lasting values in the hills. Ah, to retreat to the mountains! It is the dream of many city dwellers caught in the frantic pace of modern life. No more subways. No more muggings. No more polluted air. No more traffic. The certain strength of the hills is what we seek.

The psalmist is not so easily fooled. He knows that the permanence of nature is an illusion. The hills change. Even hills with sanctuaries on top of them are not a permanent refuge. Fire, storm, avalanche, erosion, earthquake. If not in this generation, then in some future generation, "every mountain and hill" shall "be made low" (Isa. 40:4). The hills raise the question of eternity, but they do not provide the substance of eternity.

> My help comes from the Lord,
> who made heaven and earth.
> (Ps. 121:2)

"My help." The first person singular is significant. The psalmist is not talking about help in abstract terms. This is help for me. For the particular person I am with my eyes focused on the hills, with my own anxiety about death and permanence, with my own intense desire for "help." God addresses me directly: "My help comes from the Lord."

Prayer is highly personal theological reflection. Prayer is pondering the issue of what truth shall be the foundation of my life and dispensing with all false answers and settling on God alone.

Deciding on God does not negate the power and beauty of the hills. God "made heaven and earth." Faith intensifies the experience of nature's grandeur. The hills become valuable for more than themselves. The hills are the symbol of God's majesty and permanence. It is no wonder that the ancients built their sanctuaries at the top of peaks. I shall lift up my eyes to the hills over and over because they are the continual reminder of the Lord who created them.

Prayer is viewing the natural world as a sign of God's greatness. Prayer is using the sight of hills or any other natural phenomenon to lead us to faith. Prayer is discovering that the cosmic force of the universe is the power that can personally help us.

> He will not let your foot be moved,
>   he who keeps you will not slumber.
> Behold, he who keeps Israel
>   will neither slumber nor sleep.
>   (Ps. 121:3–4)

These verses shift from the pronoun "my" to "your." The change may represent the voice of a new speaker, such as a priest addressing a pilgrim who has journeyed up the hill to the temple.

The change in pronouns could represent something else. It could stand for the psalmist's realization that God is not only *my* help. God also helps others. In the excitement of prayer the psalmist pictures himself declaring to people how God will help them. The psalmist may in the future actually make a public witness of faith. For the time being he makes it in prayer.

A father once told me: "I have prayed that my children would find God in their life. I have prayed as if God and they and I are all gathered together and I am introducing them to God, who has meant so much to me."

What happened to the psalmist and to the father may happen to us. We experience God's help, and it is such a good and freeing thing that we want to share it with others. Debate about whether or not to be evangelical ceases when someone discovers that "my help comes from the Lord." Prayer impels us to make known the most stirring truth of our existence. Prayer makes us ready to open our faith to others.

The psalmist's way of explaining his belief is instructive to all who would share their faith. The psalmist does not clout his listener with his own experience of God's grandeur. The psalmist starts at a more elementary level. He gives two simple examples: walking and sleeping.

We all have known the awkwardness of tripping when we were walking along the sidewalk or stepping out of the door. How often at a wedding rehearsal I have heard the bride say, "I hope I don't trip when I walk up the chancel steps." And students at commencement will mutter, "If only I don't stumble when I go to get my diploma."

Bodily coordination is taken as a sign of inner grace. Physical awkwardness is a symbol of interior fumbling. We do not want to stumble and fall as we walk through life. The psalmist shapes his message of faith so that it speaks to our fundamental human fear of falling down: "He will not let your foot be moved."

The psalmist also knows how scary the night is. Children often want a parent in the bedroom to help them fall asleep. Not to read a story or to get a glass of water. But just to be there. Adults never completely outgrow this childhood desire to know that someone is keeping watch while they sleep. The desire is especially acute in times of crisis and illness. Chaplains in hospitals and nurses on night duty often speak of how patients grow restless during the hours of dark.

Prayer is discovering in the middle of insomnia that "he who keeps Israel will neither slumber nor sleep." Prayer is sinking into a good night's rest with the knowledge that God is always fully awake.

> The Lord is your keeper;
>   the Lord is your shade
>   on your right hand.
> The sun shall not smite you by day,
>   nor the moon by night.

> (Ps. 121:5–6)

The psalmist turns to the imagery of the courtroom. The phrase "your shade on your right hand" may indicate where the defendant of an accused person stood during a trial (Oxford Study Edition of *The New English Bible,* 1976).

Each of us stands accused in life. That is how we feel sometimes. We think it is up to us to justify our existence. If we fail, then blindly impersonal forces, represented in the psalm by "the sun" and "the moon," shall "smite" us. We have not done enough good. We are not a success. We are not "somebody important." We have failed to measure up to the standards of our culture, and the jury, consisting of society and our secret inner voices, renders a verdict of "guilty."

Prayer is discovering that the verdict is not as we feared. There is a witness in the case who we thought would be an accuser. This one figure has more grounds than anyone else to condemn us. But instead of pleading against us, this one figure is our defendant: "If God is for us, who is against us? . . . It is God who justifies; who is to condemn?" (Rom. 8:31ff.).

Prayer is the joyful shout of the accused when the verdict is, "Not guilty." Prayer is knowing that our life is no longer strangled by guilt and crushed by judgment. All the bogeymen of uncertainty that gossip about our failure and point the condemning finger are hushed up. God is on our side. God is our "keeper" and our "shade" at our "right hand."

> The Lord will keep you from all evil;
>   he will keep your life.
> The Lord will keep
>   your going out and your coming in
>   from this time forth and for evermore.
>   (Ps. 121:7–8)

There are days when we are so busy that "we don't know whether we're going or coming." Life reaches a feverish pace where the primary fact of existence is not what we are doing but simply doing. We rush from the dry cleaner's to the tennis lesson to the doctor's to the school to the job to the meeting to the store to the concert to the neighbor's. Home is no longer our street address or our apartment number. Our residence is simply one more place where we drop in and out. Home is our going and our coming. We live in the midst of activity, and particular locations are only temporary stopping points.

Some of this busyness is unhealthy escape. It is keeping on the run in order to avoid the hollow silence of our souls.

But sometimes the busyness of life is not escape. Circumstance demands that we run. Someone is hurting. Someone is asking us to serve. Someone has a cause that deserves support. Someone is demanding our attention. And all these someones need us at the same time. What happens then? Do we panic and give up on prayer because we shall never have the solitude we think we need for finding God? The psalmist doesn't.

The psalmist knows that when he returns from the hills, when he leaves the sanctuary behind, he will not be leaving God behind. God will be with him. The most demanding schedules of common life never take us outside of God's watch. God is our "dwelling place" (Ps. 90:1), the One in whom "we live and move and have our being" (Acts 17:28).

Prayer is staying in touch with God while we are on the run.

Prayer is not necessarily words. We may be so busy telling our children what time we will pick them up that we can't be talking to God. Nevertheless, we are aware that the boundaries of God's care are always greater than the perimeters of daily life. This awareness is our prayer. It is the psalmist's realization that "the Lord will keep your going out and your coming in."

Some goings and comings are greater than others. Going away to school. Going away to the service. Going away to one's first job. Going away to be married. Going to the hospital. Going the way of all flesh. They are all much greater than going to the store for milk and eggs. They make us shake inside.

To leave our "country" and our "kindred" and our "father's house" (Gen. 12:1) for some unknown territory can be a fearful thing. What will it be like there? Will it be like home? Will I be accepted? Will I be able to make it on my own? Will I know anyone there? Or will I be entirely alone and forgotten and ignored? The psalmist may be haunted by these fears, but if he is, they never overwhelm him. Greater than his fear is his faith: "The Lord will keep you from all evil; he will keep your life."

Prayer is being grasped by a hope more powerful than our greatest anxiety.

"Coming in" is a more comfortable act than "going out." My colleague, Richard Manzelmann, points out that "coming in" to the world, birth, is the natural occasion of joy for a family. "Going out," death, is the occasion of grief and fear.

To "come in" from the storm. To "come in" to the church. To "come in" from our work. All sound reassuring and soothing.

Yet "coming in" can be difficult. How do we readjust to home after so many years of a different life-style? How do we return to the Christian fellowship after so much skepticism and private searching? How do we reclaim values that we have rejected during a period of personal confusion? How do we do these things and not get swamped with feelings of embarrassment and failure? Painful questions with no easy answers.

One thing is clear: the Lord will watch over our coming in as well as our going out. Prayer is the inner struggle through which this belief becomes our personal conviction. Prayer is the tortured process which makes us realize that to lose face is less devastating than to lose faith. Prayer is the terrible moment of coming to our senses and deciding, "I will arise and go to my father, and I will say to him, 'Father, I have sinned against heaven and before you' " (Luke 15:18). Prayer is confession followed by the glad discovery that God sees us starting back home and runs and embraces us before we arrive (Luke 15:20). God guards our "coming in."

God is not like the parent who grows tired of answering the door and tells the restless children: "Now this is your last chance. Either come in and stay, or go out and play. I'm not coming to the door again." God will always come to the door again. Parents should not feel judged by this. After all, they are human. But God is God and never gets tired of answering the door. God stands there continually to guard us whether we are going out or coming in "from this time forth and for evermore."

God's help and protection are grand theological themes. Still they don't add up to a blessed thing if we repeat them as clichés and fail to experience them as realities. Prayer is the way to that experience. It is not an experience which always starts by shutting out the distractions of the world.

Bowing our heads and closing our eyes is not the only posture for prayer. The psalmist first "lifts up" his eyes to the hills before he asks the question, "From whence does my help come?" The visual world instigates the exploration of the invisible truth of God.

Looking at the world is not a passive effort. It demands energy. Lifting one's eyes suggests something greater than merely glancing at one's surroundings. It is too often true of us that we "see and see, but do not perceive" (Isa. 6:9).

Prayer is perception. It is looking at nature so intensely that one experiences the world as the creation of God. Prayer transforms the image on our retinas into the interior vision of faith. We look at the world and see heaven.

Prayer is the process of moving from the sight of hills to the personal conviction that God cares about us. The psalmist was aided in this process by a ritual. He climbed a hill to a sanctuary. The outward physical act nurtured the interior journey of the soul.

We need to reclaim the psalmist's ritual. This does not involve building all our churches on hilltops! It means perceiving the world as a sacred sign.

We can look at a hill or a mountain ritually, as though we were making a pilgrimage to a sanctuary at its top. We begin to climb and to feel the quickening pulse of our hearts. We reflect on the power that folded rock and earth into awesome shapes. We question if we'll make it all the way, yet we are drawn irresistibly toward the top.

As we set a pace and rise to higher ground and sense the strength of the mountain, we wonder, "From whence does my help come?" The question settles into our stride. It is a part of every step we take toward the sanctuary at the top. Then we break our rhythm to dash over the last few yards. There is a rush of power; we know that "help comes from the Lord, who made heaven and earth." Our belief is punctuated by our arrival. We hear a priestly voice confirm the pilgrimage of faith: "He will not let your foot be moved, he who keeps you will not slumber."

When we return, there is a certainty about our prayerful ascent that we did not have when we started from the base of the mountain. We descend to the valley with the glad assurance that "the Lord will keep your going out and your coming in from this time forth and for evermore."

It is not necessary that one's private journey follow the route that I have imagined. The vital thing is to nurture a sacramental vision of the world. This may involve imaginary rituals of perception in which we start simply with an object and slowly make our way to the greater reality of God.

The ancient pilgrim climbed step by step to the temple on the hill. We too can move step by step to God.

We look at the hills.

We reflect on their permanence and our transience.

We consider that even nature at its most enduring is not eternal.

We turn to the power of the Creator.

In all of this we are praying. For prayer is the skeleton of logic, fleshed out by experience, and animated by faith. Prayer fulfills the desires of reason for meaning and wholeness. In prayer we dare to discover what our reason wishes to believe and our eyes long to see.

As we walk toward the truth, there is One who walks with us and who will not let our "foot be moved." One who will keep our "going out" and our "coming in from this time forth and for evermore."

7

Collapse of a Nation

Everything the man loved was being destroyed. Everything he cherished was mocked. Every value, every institution that he had trusted in was shaken. When he saw the flag burned, the same flag he had fought under in the Pacific, it made him weep. Decency, respect, patriotism, faith, marriage. All were up for grabs. Nothing was sacred.

The man's world was collapsing. His disorientation and shock were the same as that of the psalmist who witnessed the destruction of the holy temple in Jerusalem:

> O God, why dost thou cast us off for ever?
> Why does thy anger smoke against the sheep
> of thy pasture?
>
> (Ps. 74:1)

"Cast off for ever" by God. That is exactly how we feel when our private worlds crumble. We build meaning into life by attaching significance to certain institutions and objects. For the psalmist the key symbol of value was the temple; for the man it was everything that he associated with the "American way of life." When these symbols were attacked, the meaning they provided was shaken. Since God is considered the ultimate source and sustainer of life's meaning, it seemed as though God had "cast off" the very people who had honored the divinely appointed symbols of God's grace and power.

The psalmist, however, does not analyze his situation. His shock is too severe for calm reflection. He feels a devastating finality to the terror that has overtaken Israel. It is not as though God has just stepped out for the moment. God has cast them off "for ever"!

"For ever" may seem an exaggeration to those who think of God's mercy as everlasting. But the period during which a person's world collapses appears to mark the end of time and the beginning of eternity. It seems as though the consequences will last "for ever." The grieving widow says, "I shall never be able to live without him." The patient in pain asks, "Will the doctor never get here?" The man weeping over the burnt flag wonders, "What is this world coming to?" In each case it feels as though God has "cast us off for ever."

The psalmist takes God's rejection personally. "Why does thy anger smoke against the sheep of thy pasture?" The smoke from the burning temple is more than the product of combustion. It is a visual sign that God has turned against the psalmist and Israel. The smoke suffocates the psalmist's relationship to God because it is clear evidence to the psalmist that God is directly responsible for Israel's catastrophe.

The psalmist's feeling that God has it in for Israel is the common reaction of all people undergoing upheaval in their lives. "Why did God do this to me?" Christians should not be so eager to proclaim God's love that they ignore this question. To do so is to cut off the possibility of an honest confrontation with God. Rather than pretend feelings of satisfaction with God, people should be free to argue with God.

The psalmist does not take God's rejection lying down. The psalmist fights back. He challenges God by recalling God's promises:

> Remember thy congregation, which thou
>   hast gotten of old,
> which thou hast redeemed to be the
>   tribe of thy heritage!
> Remember Mount Zion, where thou hast dwelt.
>   (Ps. 74:2)

The psalmist throws in God's face the very vows of faithfulness that God said would be kept with Israel. The psalmist does not stop to reflect on Israel's failures, but argues only one side of the question, his human feelings of abandonment and unfairness. It is all right to pray in this way. God does not insist that all prayer start from a balanced perspective on who is right and who is wrong. If we feel that God has dealt unfairly with us, God is ready to hear our complaint.

Prayer is wrestling with God. Prayer is taking on, not the heavyweight champion of the world, but the ruler of the universe! It is pitting ourselves against God Almighty. It is stretching every tendon and tensing every muscle of the soul in a no-holds-barred struggle with the Lord. Paul said, "Fight the good fight of the faith" (I Tim. 6:12), not "Dance the lovely dance of faith."

Fight. That is what the psalmist does and what many people in the Bible do. Abraham does not complacently accept God's decision to destroy Sodom, but bargains with the Almighty to spare the city for the sake of ten righteous people (Gen. 18:22–33). Jacob wrestles with God and has the temerity to say, "I will not let you go, unless you bless me" (Gen. 32:26). Moses argues God out of striking the rebellious Israelites with a pestilence and disinheriting them (Num. 14:11–20). And Christ himself first asks, "Let this cup pass from me" before acquiescing with the words "not as I will, but as thou wilt" (Matt. 26:39).

Prayer is not simple submission to God's will. Unfortunately some Christians make it sound this way, and thereby stop people from leveling with God.

A nun once told me of a young woman who survived an automobile accident in which her fiancé was killed. When the woman awoke in the intensive care unit to hear the news, she turned against God. Her life had been difficult, and she had only found faith through personal struggle and through the guidance of this wonderful nun.

The woman now raged against God. God had taken away the one man who had loved and respected her.

Shortly after the accident the nun called on the woman and found her more distraught than before. A clergyman had visited the woman and chastised her for not accepting God's will. The nun assured the woman that it was all right to rage against God. The nun knew that the woman had to have someone to blame. She needed a target for her anger. The nun told how the psalmists have it out with God and then work their way back to peace with God. The woman found great relief in this. She blamed God, until slowly with the nun's help it broke upon her that perhaps God was not at fault.

At long last the woman felt reconciled to God and started to rebuild her life. This was largely the result of the genuine prayer which the nun nurtured in the woman. It was the same authentic expression that we find in the psalmist: "Why does thy anger smoke against the sheep of thy pasture? . . . Remember Mount Zion, where thou hast dwelt."

The psalmist tells God what to do: "Direct thy steps to the perpetual ruins" (Ps. 74:3). There is no hesitation on the psalmist's part to give God advice. The psalmist does not reflect: "I am a mere mortal and you are divine. Who am I to order you around?" Rather, the psalmist speaks to God as if God were his servant: "Direct thy steps." Do what I command, God.

The psalmist is sinning. He is reversing roles with God, and that is sin. Prayer can be an act of sin. This sounds preposterous at first, but it must be said. If prayer is to be a faultless, holy act, then no human being can pray.

We think we know better than God. If we try to hide this, if we pretend to believe that God is always right, then we only compound our sin with hypocrisy.

God does stupid, foolish things. At least that is how it appears to anyone who takes life seriously. Innocent people suffer and die. Children starve. A young man engaged to be married is killed in an automobile accident. Earthquakes swallow whole villages. God's temple is pillaged. All abstract theory about God's wisdom and justice crumbles when we experience these things. We become like the psalmist, ready to tell God what ought to be done.

Prayer is commanding God how to act. Prayer is saying: "Do this, God."

God will not necessarily obey us, anymore than a parent responds to every demand that a child makes. But God does let us speak our piece. God even expects it of us. God can more easily tolerate our attempts at being commander and chief of the universe than our attempts at being the perfectly righteous priest.

No conversation is more strained than when someone who is furious with us acts as though nothing were wrong. His very politeness galls us. When we are angry with heaven, assumed piety is abhorrent to God. God prefers honest anger to counterfeit humility.

The psalmist tries to coerce God into action by laying out before God just how terrible the destruction is:

> Thy foes have roared in the midst of thy holy place;
>   they set up their own signs for signs.
> At the upper entrance they hacked
>   the wooden trellis with axes.
> And then all its carved wood
>   they broke down with hatchets and hammers.
> They set thy sanctuary on fire;
>   to the ground they desecrated the dwelling place
>   of thy name.
> They said to themselves, "We will utterly
>   subdue them";
>   they burned all the meeting places of God
>   in the land.
>
> (Ps. 74:4–8)

The psalmist wants God to see how much God's own interests are at stake. The psalmist refers to the temple as "thy holy place," "thy sanctuary," and "the dwelling place of thy name." Not for one minute does the psalmist reflect on how God never wanted a temple in the first place. When David initially suggested the idea, God's response was, "I have not dwelt in a house since the day I brought up the people of Israel from Egypt" (II Sam. 7:6). The temple was a concession on God's part to fill Israel's need for a permanent visual symbol of God's presence. It was not God who needed a "house of cedar" (II Sam. 7:7), but Israel.

Now, however, as the temple burns, the psalmist talks as if destruction of the sanctuary were synonymous with the destruction of what is most vital to God. The psalmist identifies his own system of meaning and value with God's. The psalmist confuses his human perspective with God's divine vision.

The psalmist's confusion is a common characteristic of urgent prayer. We assume that our requests are the same as God's desires. Our need is God's need. That is the unquestioned assumption of much prayer that issues out of personal distress.

The vividness of our experience reinforces our assumption. The psalmist has a sharp image of the temple's destruction. He has heard the sounds of ax blades ringing in the temple as they usually do in the forest. He has been terrified to see the enemy hack to pieces something that was precious and beautiful and significant.

There are times in prayer when we shall be as heartsick as the psalmist. All that we can dwell on is our loss, our pain. This is the devastation of prayer, prayer that gets stuck in our own situation. There is no easy way out.

The psalmist handles his predicament by moving from a consideration of the temple's physical destruction to the deeper spiritual crisis that engulfs Israel:

> We do not see our signs;
>> there is no longer any prophet,
>> and there is none among us who knows how long.
> How long, O God, is the foe to scoff?
>> Is the enemy to revile thy name for ever?
> Why dost thou hold back thy hand,
>> why dost thou keep thy right hand in thy bosom?
>
>   (Ps. 74:9–11)

Here is the real terror: there is no way to make sense out of what is happening. It is bad enough to see the temple destroyed. But even worse is that there is no one who can provide some explanation, some understanding of what has taken place. There is no "prophet," no one who can declare what the limits of suffering are and tell how even tragedy can fit into God's purpose. Nothing is more devastating than meaninglessness. Suffering is always hard, but meaningless suffering is the hardest of all.

It is the absurdity of the modern world that crushes people more than any one political or financial crisis. Like the psalmist, "we do not see our signs; there is no longer any prophet." We seem to be the plaything of powers that have run insanely out of control. It appears as though primeval chaos is swallowing up the order and security of a world that once made sense to us.

The psalmist formerly believed that the forces of chaos were under control. He recalls:

> Yet God my King is from of old,
>   working salvation in the midst of the earth.
> Thou didst divide the sea by thy might;
>   thou didst break the heads of the dragons
>   on the waters.
> Thou didst crush the heads of Leviathan,
>   thou didst give him as food for the creatures
>   of the wilderness.
> Thou didst cleave open springs and brooks;
>   thou didst dry up ever-flowing streams.
>
> (Ps. 74:12–15)

The "dragons," "waters," and "Leviathan" are symbols of the darkest, most fearful forces in existence. They represent those powers which are opposed to the order of the universe and the meaning of life. God subdued the evil powers in the past. God conquered them at the creation of the world and at the crossing of the Red Sea and the Jordan River. This is the very meaning of the word "salvation" (v. 12): God is victorious over the chaos that would destroy us. The psalmist has believed this. It has been his faith as it was the faith of his ancestors.

The psalmist finds evidence to vindicate his faith in the order of the natural world:

> Thine is the day, thine also the night;
>   thou hast established the luminaries
>   and the sun.
> Thou hast fixed all the bounds of the earth;
>   thou hast made summer and winter.
>
> (Ps. 74:16–17)

Turning to nature in the face of chaotic human events is not peculiar to the psalmist. It is characteristic of our own age. The back-to-earth movement, the popularity of camping, the boom in mountain climbing and vacation homes are more than the luxuries of a consumer society. They are efforts to reestablish contact with

the fundamental structure of the universe. They are the prayer of
the psalmist who finds in the ordered ways of nature the regularity
and meaning that have been shot to pieces by history. We must not
make fun of this prayer. It represents the irrepressible human
yearning to find some clear evidence of a force that is greater than
the powers of chaos.

But no retreat to nature can fill the hole left by catastrophic
events in the world of human affairs. After a lull of contemplating
the ordinary wonders of night and day, summer and winter, the
psalmist's anguish returns. He fires at God a fresh volley of impetu-
ous pleas:

> Remember this, O Lord, how the enemy scoffs,
>   and an impious people reviles thy name.
> Do not deliver the soul of thy dove to the
>   wild beasts;
>   do not forget the life of thy poor for ever.
> Have regard for thy covenant;
>   for the dark places of the land are full
>   of the habitations of violence.
> Let not the downtrodden be put to shame;
>   let the poor and needy praise thy name.
>   (Ps. 74:18–21)

The fever and the urgency which marked the psalmist's initial
requests have returned. Prayer is like that. It has a certain pace and
rhythm. Anguish and peace. Peace and anguish. Prayer is like
waiting for breakers at the seashore. A tremendous crashing wave
is followed by a long withdrawing roar and the lapping of white
foam and the stillness of water gathering in the hollows of rock and
sand. Then again, a tremendous crashing wave! If we would pray
as genuinely as the psalmist, we must know the waters that surround our life. We must brace ourselves for their most rugged
assaults and stand relaxed in their gentlest splashing.

The psalmist has not abandoned his old ways of manipulating
God into action. The psalmist commands God: "Have regard for
thy covenant." Yet not a word passes the psalmist's lips about how
Israel has broken the covenant. There is deception here as there can

be in all prayer. We must never forget that. We must not only pray but also look at our prayer and find what hidden distortions are a part of our very words to God. Prayer then becomes insight into the depths of our character. We discover that in the godly act of prayer we may be our most godless. Prayer reveals our sin.

The psalmist is not above using the relief he found in nature to urge God to act in history: "Do not deliver the soul of thy dove to the wild beasts." The phrase "wild beasts" picks up the earlier imagery of the mad forces that God has tamed in nature. Since God has conquered the ferocious monsters of nature, surely God can see fit to do the same for God's "dove," Israel.

God does not answer the psalmist. So once again the psalmist hurls his heart against heaven:

> Arise, O God, plead thy cause;
>> remember how the impious scoff at thee
>> all the day!
> Do not forget the clamor of thy foes,
>> the uproar of thy adversaries which goes
>> up continually!
>
> (Ps. 74:22–23)

The psalmist pictures the world as a great courtroom. God has been charged with failing to uphold the divine end of a contract between heaven and earth. God is in default. There is an abundance of witnesses against God. The "uproar" of God's "adversaries . . . goes up continually." There is none to present God's case. Only God can do that. The psalmist begs that God step into the court, that God indicate the divine cause and defeat those who "scoff at thee all the day."

God never shows up. At least never in Psalm 74. No answer. No messenger. No defense. Nothing. This is the most shattering moment of prayer. To know with all our hearts that God is on our side, that our cause is just, and yet to hear nothing from God. To be left suspended between faith and terror. "It cannot be," we say. "God answers prayer. God will come, we know God will come." Let anyone who thinks this way read Psalm 74. God does not always come. God does not always answer prayer. God is not hired help to do whatever we request. God is God!

God is so great that the apparent destruction of everything that stands for God is not cause enough to make heaven speak if it is not in God's heart to do so. God does not have to respond on our terms. We can plead. We can manipulate. We can beg. God will never—absolutely never—reject us for doing any of these things. But that does not mean God will give the answer we want. God loves us too much to give us every desire of our hearts and to confirm us in our false securities. Not the temple, not our theology, not our prayers are great enough to contain God's purpose and to define God's will.

Psalm 74 tells us to rage against God when rage we must. Pull out every stop. Use every argument. Make every point we can to prove that our position is fair and right. But be prepared for silence. Be ready for the fearful revelation that we are flesh and the Lord alone is God.

Psalm 74 is not satisfying to a generation who thinks there must be an answer or a technique to solve every problem. We are spoiled by our technology. We flip a switch to get light. We dial a number to talk with a friend. We use a pocket calculator to do our computations. The physical world is at our fingertips and so we assume that God is. We have a push-button mentality which pervades our faith.

Our questions about prayer reveal the technological orientation of our religious understanding: Does prayer work? Does God answer prayer? We speak as though prayer were a matter of building an electrical circuit to plug into the Spirit or as though it were a question of writing a computer program that would get God to feed out answers.

Prayer is much messier than our inventions. There is no formula, no program, no technique, no theory, no combination of all these that will make prayer "work," that will get God to "answer."

Prayer is any attempt to address God. The final outcome of prayer is not known in advance. If it were, it would not be prayer. It would be an inner monologue designed to cover a purely human decision with a blanket of sanctity.

God does sometimes "answer" prayer. We receive clear guid-

ance or direct response to our concern. When this happens, we feel
that prayer "works." However, prayer does not always follow this
pattern. Sometimes prayer ends the way Psalm 74 does. Then the
strength of our faith and the resilience of our prayer life are put
to the test.

The courageous thing about the psalmist is his persistence. He
does not give up. Nor does he turn to feeble religious clichés about
accepting God's will. The psalmist takes both life and God too
seriously to be satisfied with cheap religious answers.

Frequently prayer appears to be a weak and sentimental act
because the psalmist's simultaneous concern for both life and God
is missing. If we take life seriously and God lightly, then our
prayers will lack the psalmist's clear direction. We will be confused
about whom we are addressing. The psalmist has none of this
uncertainty. He is speaking to God and to none other.

If we take life lightly and God seriously, then our prayers will
be namby-pamby. Our pleas to heaven will be insipid, and prayer
will be the unctuous flattery that turns away many secular people.
The psalmist has none of this pretentious piety. He cares desper-
ately about what is happening and will not let God easily off the
hook.

It is the psalmist's dual commitment to the world and to God
that makes his prayer powerful. The psalm hides nothing of his
humanity. It reveals a passionate relationship to God. This is genuine prayer. Not slick, not religious, not smooth, but genuine.

How wonderful that there is a God who will let us struggle this
openly against heaven. Surely this is a God of love. A God who
places in Holy Scripture an unanswered prayer is a God who can
be trusted. If every prayer in the Bible received a perfect response,
the Bible would be suspect. That's not the way life is. We would
wonder what God was trying to pull over on us. Instead, we
discover that God understands. God knows that there are times
when, from a human perspective, we seem to be left hanging between terror and faith. It is part of being a person.

The fact that God understands our predicament indicates that
someday there will be a resolution. "For now we see in a mirror
dimly," but at a future point we "shall understand fully" even as

we "have been fully understood" (I Cor. 13:12). There will come a time when God will arise to "plead" the "cause" of heaven. Then the "uproar" of God's "adversaries" will be stilled, and the fires of anguish cooled, and all people will meet the truth "face to face" (I Cor. 13:12).

8

Going Home

They married just before the Air Force stationed them overseas. She had never been away from home, and it was traumatic for her even to think of leaving behind her family. But they were very much in love. She was sure that "simply being together" would compensate for any homesickness.

Things did not work out that way.

She was miserable. The plasterboard apartment, the bland gaudiness of the PX, the strangeness of a country whose language she did not know and whose people seemed indifferent made her yearn for home.

The usual problems of a new marriage were all credited to this one cause: being so far from family and friends and accustomed surroundings.

The couple applied for a transfer back to the States. They wanted the base that was twenty miles from their parents, but they would take anything that would at least put them closer to home.

They waited and then waited some more. Every letter from the folks intensified their impatience. It seemed as though they would never return home.

Then the transfer came through. They were moving to the very post they had requested.

Their spirits soared like a skyrocket. God had answered their prayers. They felt as the ancient Israelites had upon returning from exile in Babylon to their homeland:

> When the Lord restored the fortunes of Zion,
>   we were like those who dream.
> Then our mouth was filled with laughter,

and our tongue with shouts of joy;
then they said among the nations,
  "The Lord has done great things for them."
The Lord has done great things for us;
  we are glad.

(Ps. 126:1–3)

Everything was looking up. Life was about to start again. They were going home.

Back to the familiar sights.

Back to what they loved.

Back to what they had dreamed about and yearned for.

That is how the Israelites felt; that is how the young couple felt. They were returning to the lost paradise, to the sacred land, to home. Everything would be all right once again.

For several weeks the couple relived the past. They visited their former haunts. They saw a few old friends. They had their favorite meals with their folks. They reveled in being home.

Then the bloom of enthusiasm faded. The couple met a friend at the shopping plaza. She was pushing a carriage filled with groceries and a baby. Her husband had run away, and she was left juggling a job, a child, car payments, and a landlord who wanted her out of the flat. She had been a cheerleader four years ago. Now she was fat and sour. The couple edged away from her for fear of catching the blight that had sapped her vivacity and made her old while she was young.

Other friends were doing well, but most of them were gone. They came home occasionally for a weekend. Then there was a glad reunion, and old times sparkled as brightly as the ice cubes in their mixed drinks. But Monday morning, when the couple opened the refrigerator and saw the leftovers of Saturday night's meal in a restaurant doggie bag, they knew that the home they had dreamed of was not the home they were living in.

That home did not exist. It was a myth, a paradise of the imagination to which they escaped from the pains of marriage and of growing up. They had tried to make the myth real. They had returned only to discover that the place of their origins was no more home to them than the land overseas. Home had vanished.

The Israelites went through the same disillusionment when they returned from Babylon. The writer of Psalm 126 does not describe the poverty and destruction which they found, but we know from Ezra and Nehemiah that the holy land was in a sorry state: "The survivors there in the province [of Judah] who escaped exile are in great trouble and shame; the wall of Jerusalem is broken down, and its gates are destroyed by fire" (Neh. 1:3).

The holy city for which the exiles wept (Ps. 137) had become a dump. The glorious land they had dreamed of was not the home they returned to. In their disappointment they turned to God:

> Restore our fortunes, O Lord,
>   like the watercourses in the Negeb!
> May those who sow in tears
>   reap with shouts of joy!
> He that goes forth weeping,
>   bearing the seed for sowing,
> shall come home with shouts of joy,
>   bringing his sheaves with him.
> (Ps. 126:4–6)

Prayer is dealing with our disillusionment. It is turning in desperation to God and seeking the intervention of heaven.

The psalmist indicates his desire for instant relief by asking that Israel's fortunes be restored "like the watercourses in the Negeb." These were the stream beds in the south that were usually dry but filled up suddenly with a mighty rush of water during the rainy season. The psalmist wants just as dramatic a change in Israel's situation.

Once the psalmist makes his initial demand, his tone shifts. The simile changes from a flash flood to a sower, from instant intervention to a process of growth.

The psalmist describes the sower as "weeping" (v. 6). The psalmist now knows that Israel must go ahead with the task of rebuilding life even though the nation is still sad and disillusioned. The power to do this comes from the conviction that God will bring Israel's efforts to a fruitful conclusion. The sower who goes out weeping "shall come home with shouts of joy, bringing his sheaves with him." The psalmist has not given up hope of God's flash flood. Only now the psalmist realizes what efforts he must make to prepare for God's watering.

When the Air Force wife first saw me, she was like the psalmist. She wanted a flash flood. She wanted her dry existence instantly transformed. But once she had gotten this request out into the open, then the struggle that lay before her became clear. There would be no sudden change. She and her husband would have to start from where they were. While they were still "weeping," while they were still disillusioned with the move back home, they had to begin working on their marriage and their adulthood.

Prayer is moving from an impossible expectation to a realistic hope. The impossible expectation is that the universe can be refashioned into the womb from which we came. The realistic hope is that our sorrow can be reshaped into joy.

Prayer starts with our most extravagant demands. The woman knew this. She had prayed over and over that she and her husband would be sent home. When the excitement of moving back withered, she prayed that something more would happen. In the process of praying and living and waiting, it dawned on her that she had to do something. She had to find help. If she did, she knew that somehow things would work out. This awareness of the need to take some action was the answer to her prayer. "In tears" (v. 5) she came seeking counsel.

Prayer is facing up to life. It is leaving behind our nostalgia and looking squarely at the present and the future. Prayer is realizing that God who waters even the desert will also give growth to us. Prayer is planting the seed of hope in the midst of our devastated lives and knowing, as did the psalmist, that one day we shall have a garden.

9

Thunderstorm

The storm moved closer. It had started about a mile down the valley. I had been counting five seconds between each flash of lightning and crash of thunder, but now I was down to three seconds. Then two. Then the air cracked above us. It sounded as though a colossal ax had, with one splintering stroke, split our apartment house down the middle. We were not hit. But for several minutes heaven tried to cleave the earth in two. The storm moved on and its sharp crashes returned to the less threatening roll of celestial kettledrums.

"Did you ever understand those explanations of lightning we learned in earth science?" asked my friend.

"Something about positive and negative charges building up and leaping to each other. That's about what I remember. And also how it's necessary for the nitrogen cycle and the ozone layer."

"I've always thought that in some ways the ancients' theory made more sense. There are heavenly beings at war or God is speaking. When a storm comes over us, as it did just now, it seems to be more personal than an electrical discharge."

My friend was talking like the psalmist who witnessed an awesome storm move inland from the Mediterranean:

> The voice of the Lord is upon the waters;
>   the God of glory thunders,
>   the Lord, upon many waters.
> The voice of the Lord is powerful,
>   the voice of the Lord is full of majesty.
> The voice of the Lord breaks the cedars,
>   the Lord breaks the cedars of Lebanon.
> He makes Lebanon to skip like a calf,

and Sirion like a young wild ox.
The voice of the Lord flashes forth flames
    of fire.
The voice of the Lord shakes the wilderness,
    the Lord shakes the wilderness of Kadesh.
The voice of the Lord makes the oaks to whirl,
    and strips the forests bare;
    and in his temple all cry, "Glory!"

(Ps. 29:3–9)

The psalmist experiences the storm as a personal manifestation of God's power. In our more rational moments we tend to look down at the psalmist. His is the primitive perception of an age that lacked our scientific understanding. We may enjoy the psalmist's poetic imagery, but a precise knowledge of electrical discharge is more valuable in our purview than the psalmist's description of lightning as "the voice of the Lord [which] flashes forth flames of fire."

The haughtiness with which we assess the psalmist reveals our own primitivism. We think we are sophisticated because of our scientific accomplishments. But we display the crudest and narrowest of sensibilities when we limit our perception of reality to what is physically understandable. The impersonal, objective stance which empowers science to make its great discoveries also weakens its ability to speak to our highly personal encounter with the universe.

"I've always thought that in some ways the ancient's theory made more sense." My friend was not rejecting science. She knew there were "explanations" for lightning that she had once been taught, and she even wanted to clarify them in her own mind. But the most perfect scientific comprehension covers only one aspect of lightning. It does not account for our experience of the storm as something that awakens personal awe and wonder.

The psalmist's perception and the scientist's explanation can be held simultaneously by the same person. They do not contradict each other. The scientist describes the finite dimensions of the phenomenon. The psalmist is confronted by the personal power behind the universe.

Prayer does not require the rejection of the scientific viewpoint. But prayer can be nurtured by recovering the psalmist's perception. How does God speak to me in the storm?

The psalmist answers the question by describing the storm's effects. The lightning, the thunder, the destruction are all experienced as direct manifestations of God.

Because of our scientific objectivity we can never totally recapture the psalmist's feeling of God's immediate, actual presence in the thunder and the lightning. Nevertheless we can probe the feelings of personal encounter which still grab us when lightning flashes over our house. We can match these feelings with the images of the psalm. Once again a thunderstorm can be the occasion of a prayer that sweeps us with a gale of Spirit as powerful as the storm outside.

Thunder is "the voice of the Lord." This reveals something about what it means to hear God speak. It indicates that God does not necessarily use words.

Thunder is heaven's eloquent reminder that life is not neatly under our control. We like to think that with a little planning and discipline we can plot our lives. The crash of thunder shakes us out of self-conplacency. It is not we who are "powerful" and "full of majesty" (v. 4) but the Lord.

Prayer is hearing thunder and realizing in a lightning flash how fragile and vulnerable life is. The wordless message rumbles with devastating clarity: My life is not my private possession. It is neither owned nor controlled nor operated by me. Life is on loan. "The Lord gives and the Lord takes away" (Job 1:21, NEB).

"The voice of the Lord breaks the cedars" (Ps. 29:5). A tree is struck by lightning. It is a scary sight. I remember as a child an enormous elm that was split in two pieces during a storm. There was a ghostly white gash down the main trunk. I stared at it and tried to calculate how long it would take to hack through the width of the tree with my boy scout ax. The lightning had cut it lengthwise in an instant!

Prayer is realizing that the same voice which breaks the trees can break us. It can break our arrogance and our selfishness. It can break our life.

Prayer is deciding that the lightning rods of self-sufficiency offer no protection against God's storm. We abandon them and acknowledge that God has good cause for striking us. God is breaking our smugness and our apathy to suffering humanity and our indolence in the cause of justice. God's voice thunders against these qualities. The voice of the Lord shatters them through prayer with the same mighty power that "breaks the cedars of Lebanon" (Ps. 29:5).

Prayer is seeing a bolt of lightning in the sky and simultaneously giving ear to the thunder that reverberates through my entire self. Prayer is listening to the voice of God break me, that I might be rebuilt into a structure worthy of the divine image which marks my essential being (Gen. 1:27).

God plucks up, breaks down, overthrows, and destroys in order to build and to plant (Jer. 31:28). The colossal electric snap of a zillion electrons reminds me of God's fearful ways. The voice of the Lord breaks before it builds. It thunders before it "speak[s] tenderly" (Isa. 40:2).

Let anyone who thinks that prayer always takes place under sunny skies and brings calm to the soul heed the psalmist: "The voice of the Lord breaks the cedars."

"The voice of the Lord shakes the wilderness, the Lord shakes the wilderness of Kadesh" (Ps. 29:8). The repeated phrases here, as in many of the other verses, capture the way thunder echoes over and over. New explosions of sound are repeated as they bounce off the mountains and rocks.

The wilderness is shaking. That's how powerful God's voice is. It causes the landscape to shudder. It also rattles the wilderness of the soul, that bleak interior space through which we wander to find meaning and purpose. It is a genuine wilderness, an untamed region of unmarked paths and unknown dangers. We frequently get lost there, turning this way and that. We try a little bit of philosophy, a little bit of political ideology, a little bit of meditation, a little bit of prayer, a little bit of psychology, a little bit of religion. None satisfies, so we keep meandering from one thing to the next, never settling down.

Then "the voice of the Lord shakes the wilderness." A wild,

white charge of electricity wallops the air above our house, and it illuminates more than the surrounding landscape. It penetrates our inner wilderness. In a flash we realize that our wandering must someday cease. We must decide where we want to head.

God is confronting us with a decision. As Israel had to decide between the golden calf and God, so we must decide what we will live for. We cannot play endlessly with the idols of the mind and the fads of society. The voice of the Lord is the inner compulsion to sort out our options in life and decide what will be the ruling priorities of our existence.

At first we hear the Lord's voice rumbling in the distance, just as the psalmist initially hears it over the Mediterranean, the "many waters" of v. 3. Next the Lord's voice moves closer as it "breaks the cedars of Lebanon" (v. 5) and makes the mountains leap (v. 6). Finally, the voice booms over the wilderness. We can put off our decision no longer, not if we would attain some degree of peace and clarity about the rest of our lives.

Prayer is responding to God in the wilderness. Prayer is seeing that a policy of making no commitments leads to the worst kind of slavery. If we refuse to bind ourselves to something or someone in particular, then we will enslave ourselves to wandering. We will be at the mercy of our disoriented desires and society's shifting fashions. We will never enter the promised land. The wilderness will be our prison.

The storm drives the psalmist to praise God. The psalmist is so excited that he urges all the other forces of the universe to recognize God's unsurpassable grandeur:

> Ascribe to the Lord, O heavenly beings,
>   ascribe to the Lord glory and strength.
> Ascribe to the Lord the glory of his name;
>   worship the Lord in holy array.
>
> (Ps. 29:1–2)

Prayer is ecstatic proclamation of God's supremacy. To quibble about the psalmist's belief in other heavenly beings is senseless. The sheer power of his experience drives the psalmist to visionary language. In the presence of God the most magnificent sights of nature pale. Canyons, mountains, oceans, stars, and sky are mere suggestions of God's majesty. Their own beauty can only serve to "ascribe to the Lord glory and strength."

The storm leaves the psalmist convinced that God is absolutely in control of the universe:

> The Lord sits enthroned over the flood;
> The Lord sits enthroned as king for ever.
>
> (Ps. 29:10)

The flood stands for the watery deep that God divided at creation (Gen. 1:1ff.). The psalmist finds in the storm evidence that the universe is sustained by the power that originally commanded, "Let the waters under the heavens be gathered together into one place, and let the dry land appear" (Gen. 1:9).

Prayer is sitting through a thunder shower and knowing that God is in control. In the midst of a storm we encounter the same power that created the world and people and pronounced them "good." That power is still here and addresses us through thunder and lightning.

Power so great that it "breaks the cedars" and makes the mountains "skip" and "shakes the wilderness" and "strips the forests bare" is power that can subdue every force that threatens to conquer us. It is power that can overcome even death.

Prayer is getting in touch with this power. It is letting a meteorological phenomenon, a thunderstorm, break open our inner selves to the driving forces of God. Prayer is asking that the power we see in the storm may sustain our own existence:

> May the Lord give strength to his people!
> May the Lord bless his people with peace!
>
> (Ps. 29:11)

Prayer is outlandishly bold. The "strength" that the psalmist requests is the same strength that was earlier ascribed to the Lord (v. 1). Prayer is asking that God's strength be shared with us! Prayer is not limited to modest requests for help and support. In prayer we dare to ask that God will lend us the power that we have witnessed firsthand in the storm. It is the only power that could conquer the natural flood (v. 10), and so we are convinced that it is the only power that can control our inner flood.

When the doctor says, "I'm sorry but the results from your lab reports are not good." When our college-age son goes out for a few beers and the state troopers come to the door at two o'clock in the morning. When we turn on the television and see children starving to death. When the family announces that our name is on a waiting list at the nursing home. When the company we've served for thirty years decides to reduce its middle management—then the flood rises inside us and around us. Then we want the power we saw in the storm. Then we pray with the psalmist, "May the Lord give strength to his people! May the Lord bless his people with peace!"

Peace. After so much breaking and thundering and shaking, peace is welcome. Yet we must not draw too distinct a line between peace and the storm. Whatever peace God gives, it will be secure, because behind it lies the same power that hurls the lightning bolt and rattles the sky.

God's peace is not the absence of might. God's peace is the presence of power. To be blessed with peace is not to live a storm-less life. It is to discover that God is stronger than any power that assaults us.

A thunderstorm is more than an electrical discharge followed by the crashing sound of disturbed air. A thunderstorm is the occasion of prayer. It is an opportunity to hear God's addressing us with power and majesty.

A storm impels us to listen to the interior turbulence of our souls. God is breaking and shaking us so that we may be blessed with an enduring peace. We do not shudder at the approach of the storm. We welcome it. We even ask for its thunderous presence:

> That I may rise and stand, o'erthrow me, and bend
> Your force, to breake, blowe, burn, and make me new.
> (John Donne, Holy Sonnets, XIV)

10

Trust

Four lanes of traffic at sixty miles an hour. Tractor-trailers, family wagons, VW bugs, sports cars, pickup trucks, and our Greyhound bus were all driving as though the highway behind them were being rolled up like carpet to be taken to the cleaners. If we didn't get out of the way fast enough, we would be rolled up with it.

Across the aisle in the bus a baby was sleeping. The mother had spread a diaper over her left shoulder and held the child there as though he were no burden at all.

The diesel's hum. Squealing brakes. Honking horns. The roar of rubber buffing concrete. Suicidal drivers who crossed without signaling from the far left-hand lane to exits on the right. None of these disturbed the child. He slept through it all.

Prayer is trusting God the way that child trusted his mother:

> But I have calmed and quieted my soul,
>> like a child quieted at its mother's breast;
>> like a child that is quieted is my soul.
>> (Ps. 131:2)

It is a lovely verse and fills us with warmth. But how does it become real for us? We are no longer babies. We are in the driver's seat now, and if we took our eyes off the road for one second, we could get clobbered by the fool who is tailgating or the moving van that wants to squeeze between us and the orange Camaro.

Life crowds us. We drive through it with the rest of the world at breakneck speed. We need to pull over and stop.

Prayer involves deliberately setting aside time to get out of life's heavy traffic. This takes discipline. We keep thinking we'll drive just a little farther through the day's routine. We will make one more phone call. We will dictate one more letter. We will get just this last thing done. Then we will take a break. But we don't. We keep driving on.

Certain types of prayer demand that we stop, that we make a conscious effort to still our revved up motors. This kind of prayer is not instigated by experiences that dramatically confront us with God's presence. Neither a close call nor a thunderstorm is the occasion for the psalmist's irenic state. His profoundly peaceful prayer does not even depend on a theological theme or a rich spiritual insight or reflection on the mysteries of God. Quite to the contrary. The psalmist has disengaged himself from any exalted vision or probing thought:

> O Lord, my heart is not lifted up,
> my eyes are not raised too high;
> I do not occupy myself with things
> too great and too marvelous for me.
>   (Ps. 131:1)

Prayer is not always strenuous. It does not always take us to the gate of heaven or lead us through shaking experiences of rebirth and wonder.

Prayer is leaning on God as a child leans on the mother's breast. This is not just a sentimental image. The psalmist describes a process that leads to the awareness of God's parental care.

"My heart is not lifted up." The psalmist sets aside his emotions. He does not seek the fervent experience of God's Spirit burning or thundering inside him. He does not request that God change his life or take away his sin or make him a new creation. There will be other times when the psalmist can deal with these desires. Then his heart will throb from wrestling with God. For now the psalmist's heart beats with the quiet pulse of one whose sleep is dreamless and secure.

Prayer is being in God's presence and knowing that we don't have to share everything we feel. As a genuine friend and a loving parent, God is glad simply to be with us. We feel the comfort of being understood without being exposed.

"My eyes are not raised too high." The psalmist does not let visual reality stun him with beauty or grandeur. He does not seek an inspiring vision. He does not become involved with his environment, but relaxes his sight.

Prayer is taking time out from our surroundings. It is reducing the visual assault of the world. It is like traveling from a tourist trap filled with neon lights to a park area where there are no signs or billboards. The visual difference can actually be sensed inside us. We do not feel so badgered and crowded by the demands of others.

Prayer is turning our three-way lamp down to 60 watts and laying aside the newspaper and being satisfied with the softer light and God's presence in the silence of the moment.

Our dimmer physical vision represents a less intense interior gaze. We do not squint the eyes of the soul, but relax and enjoy whatever gentle light shines within.

"I do not occupy myself with things too great and too marvelous for me." Prayer is not always deep. It is not always involved with the most perplexing or the most anguished questions of existence. Prayer does not always give its attention to the Bible and how God has acted in history for the salvation of humanity. Prayer can lay off the heavy stuff.

Prayer is letting the mind wander freely in the presence of God. No great revelations. No great struggles. Simple reflections that meander into fantasies and evaporate into reveries.

Prayer is the sense of unembarrassed security that we have as we doze in our favorite easy chair. Prayer is daydreaming on God's shoulder. If we cannot relax this much around God, then we have yet to perceive just how loving God is.

The mother on the bus knew that her child needed to sleep. She meanwhile kept reading and got up twice to let the passenger next to the window in and out of his seat. All the time the child rested soundly on her shoulder.

God is like that mother. God does not demand that we always give close attention to the world or to God's greatness. God knows that we need someone against whom we can lean and sleep.

Prayer is being a child in the presence of our divine parent. Just as the baby on the bus knew that the mother would not drop him, so we know that God will never drop us.

Prayer is discovering the truth of Jesus' statement that "whoever does not receive the kingdom of God like a child shall not enter it" (Mark 10:15). When we trust God "like a child quieted at its mother's breast," then we enter the kingdom. Peace. Security. Utterly dependable love. These are all ours. Not as statements of belief subject to doubt, but as the very truth of life. We rest on God with the same unquestioning trust that the child had in his mother.

The child did not feel self-conscious or awkward. He trusted because that was all he could do. There was no other option. Faith and life were of one piece for the child.

Prayer leads us to see that there is no other option for us than to trust in God. In prayer we find God to be the one absolute security of our life. We decide to put God above the aspirations of our heart, the visions of our soul, and the thoughts of our mind. We trust God more than any of these internal subjective processes, and in that act of uncalculated and unconditional trust we find serenity.

> O Israel, hope in the Lord
> from this time forth and for evermore.
>> (Ps. 131:3)

The psalmist's final verse snaps us out of our restful mood. One minute the psalmist is talking about a quiet scene between mother and child, and next he is ending his prayer with an exhortation to Israel. How can we account for the abrupt change other than understanding it as an instruction to the congregation? What inner dynamic leads from the gentle picture of maternal love to the national state?

Security. The psalmist has discovered a bedrock security in his relationship with God that makes all other claims to security seem weak and fraudulent. The trust in military power. The protection of Jerusalem's walls. The alliances with foreign powers. The national economy. All the resources that the state claims will keep us secure are seen as the undependable human contrivances which in fact they are.

Prayer does not deny the necessity of political attempts to establish the security of society. But prayer reveals the tenuous nature of every human arrangement. Prayer is discovering the flimsiness of society and the durability of God.

Hoping in the Lord is not icing to cover the cake of power politics. Hoping in the Lord is the prerequisite of sane national government. If the people of Israel first trust God "like a child quieted at its mother's breast," then they can be objective about the nation's attempts at security. They will not look to the state to provide their fundamental security as persons, since God already furnishes that. They will not deify the nation, nor expect any political organization to fulfill their basic needs for an enduring source of comfort and strength.

Prayer is seeing through the propaganda of politics. Daydreaming on God's shoulder is an act that steals the thunder from the exaggerated promises of politicians and the extraordinary claims of the state. When we "hope in the Lord from this time forth and for evermore," we look at our nation realistically. Our compromises, our alliances, our policies issue from the calm soul of a people whose most basic faith is in God. We may fail. Our nation may totter, but we will not panic, because we know that the arms which hold us will never let us go.

Children who have not been raised by dependable and loving people frequently spend much of their adult life searching for the security they lacked when young. They missed the experience of the baby on the bus who felt safe on his mother's shoulder.

The distortions of power politics may represent at a national level the same search for security that marks an individual's life. Just as the individual has not known the comfort of dependable parents, so the nation has not known the strength of God. The nation then turns exclusively to military and economic strategies, while neglecting those qualities without which a society becomes rotten at its core: integrity, justice, God's moral law.

Prayer is discovering the political significance of trusting God. Prayer frees people from the bondage of national pride by bringing them into the presence of life's only ultimate security. When a nation's people have been "calmed and quieted" by God's strength, then they know the wisdom of the psalmist's instruction, "Hope in the Lord from this time forth and for evermore."

11

Giddy Gladness

Steven had just finished taking his final freshman exam, physics. On his way back to the dorm he stopped by the post office and found a letter in his box. His girl had gotten a job at the same camp that hired him, so they would be working together for the summer.

"You would not believe! You simply would not believe! There was only one question on relativity for ten points, and the rest was a cinch. Just standard stuff on optics, electricity, and moments of force. And here, read this."

Steven shoved a ripped-open envelope into my hand, and then started fiddling with his hi-fi set. He took the two speakers off the bookcase and placed them facing outside on the windowsill. Then he went into the room next door and called me to help him carry out Jeff's stereo. He placed Jeff's set on the other windowsill, again with the speakers facing out.

Then Steven disappeared upstairs for a minute. I heard him asking someone for a record which I thought he already owned himself. When he came back down, I said, "What happened to your album of that?"

"I've still got it," he answered, while he placed the borrowed record on Jeff's changer and an identical record on his own turntable.

Next Steven turned both amplifiers to their full wattage and instructed me: "All right, when I count three, I want you to start the record on Jeff's set. I'll do the same with mine. One. Two. Three."

The synchronization was off about a second, but it didn't make any difference. The granite walls of Farnum Hall were only about sixty feet away, and the sheer volume of noise bouncing between the two buildings nearly shattered our eardrums.

Steven yelled above the sound: "It's over. I'm going home. My girl's going to be with me. I'm so happy I want to tear down the universe with sound!"

Steven's stereophonic celebration captures for an electronic age the same giddy gladness that moved the ancient worshiper to exclaim:

> Praise the Lord!
> Praise God in his sanctuary;
>   praise him in his mighty firmament!
> Praise him for his mighty deeds;
>   praise him according to his exceeding greatness!
> Praise him with trumpet sound;
>   praise him with lute and harp!
> Praise him with timbrel and dance;
>   praise him with strings and pipe!
> Praise him with sounding cymbals;
>   praise him with loud clashing cymbals!
> Let everything that breathes praise the Lord!
> Praise the Lord!
>
> (Ps. 150)

Prayer is praising God. Unfortunately, praise is something we feel awkward about. We find it difficult to accept praise and to give it. If someone praises us, we are apt to respond: "Oh you needn't say that. It really was nothing on my part." And if we go to praise other people, we fear that it will come across as flattery, as though we were trying to win their acceptance.

Because of our embarrassment, we stifle praise. We limit praise to formal expressions of gratitude and the Sunday morning prayer of adoration.

Our response to the goodness that we do find in life is often mufflled, and our relationships suffer on this account. Few human reactions are more disappointing than that of having someone we love reject our spontaneous expression of admiration. We are glad about them. Glad that they exist. Glad that they love us. Glad that they are with us, and gladdest of all when they accept our joy with appreciation and grace.

The arrangement of the Psalter is profoundly instructive in how to regain our capacity for praise. The last five psalms, Psalms 146 to 150, all open with the command: "Praise the Lord!" The raging, pleading, and crying of the earlier psalms are left behind in a crescendo of praise. The sequence of the psalms suggests the journey of faithful prayer. We praise God with joy because we have fought God with strength. We have a genuine relationship with God.

Our confrontations with God have cut loose our inhibitions about adoring God and have given us additional cause for praise. We are thankful that God was willing to listen. Part of our praise stems from amazement at God's patience and tolerance.

Corporate worship reverses the order of private prayer. The first hymn and the first prayer adore God. It is usually not until later in the service that our pressing personal concerns emerge in prayers of supplication.

Not for one minute would I suggest turning around the sequence of worship! The church gathers in response to what God has done in Jesus Christ. Glorifying and thanking God is always the first act of a worshiping congregation.

Nevertheless, people need reassurance about their personal pilgrimage through prayer. They need to hear that God does not expect feigned gladness when they are caught in the depths of sorrow. In our prayers as well as our daily life there is "a time to weep, and a time to laugh; a time to mourn, and a time to dance" (Eccl. 3:4).

Praise is the first prayer of worship and the final prayer of all faithful disciples. It is the goal toward which all other prayers move us.

Praising God is affirming the coherence of life. It is the act in which we discover and acclaim the underlying unity of the universe. The psalmist indicates this with his twofold command:

> Praise God in his sanctuary;
> praise him in his mighty firmament!

The worshiping community and the natural world blend together in a single response to God. The cosmos is God's temple. All physical phenomena join with one voice in recognizing the common source of their existence.

> Praise him for his mighty deeds;
>> praise him according to his exceeding greatness!

The "mighty deeds" are God's saving actions in history—the exodus, the giving of the law, the arrival in the promised land. The "exceeding greatness" refers to the sheer majesty of God's being. For the psalmist, action and being flow together in a unitary revelation. The psalmist finds God through both the events of history and the contemplation of existence. Moses at Mt. Sinai and the stars in the sky witness to the same God.

In a prayer of praise we abandon our distinction between the world of human events and the world of nature. We are glad for every sign of God's presence whether we see it in a newspaper story or in the first tomato from our garden. Praise is acknowledging the power that lies behind everything we see and experience.

The psalmist feels virtually no inhibitions about expressing his joy. Not once does he stop to consider whether he is laying it on a little thick. He piles praise on top of praise:

> Praise him with trumpet sound;
>> praise him with lute and harp!
> Praise him with timbrel and dance;
>> praise him with strings and pipe!
> Praise him with sounding cymbals;
>> praise him with loud clashing cymbals!
>
>> (Ps. 150:3–5)

Prayer is extravagant happiness about God. It is taking two hi-fi sets and setting the volume at full blast. Prayer is turning to music because words are inadequate.

Praising God is not always a conscious act. Absentminded whistling, singing, and humming are evidence of an irrepressible urge to give thanks despite our social conventions and feelings of embarrassment. Praise is part of our essential nature as living creatures.

> Let everything that breathes praise the Lord!
> Praise the Lord!
>
>> (Ps. 150:6)

This one verse discloses the fundamental impetus of praise: grateful astonishment at the very fact of life. We are stunned that we exist at all. Human accomplishment is nothing next to the reality of being alive. Our vision of who and what we are focuses on a single function: breathing. Not philosophizing. Not inventing. Not imagining. Not creating. But breathing defines existence. From this insight praise flows with inexorable logic and unyielding power.

Living is breathing.

Inhaling and exhaling.

We are breathing this very minute even as we have been breathing since our birth.

Inhaling and exhaling.

Every living person and every living thing is breathing.

Inhaling and exhaling.

Every motion of the diaphragm, every expansion and contraction of the lungs, is the gift of God, who breathes into our nostrils the breath of life (Gen. 2:7).

Inhaling and exhaling.

"Let everything that breathes praise the Lord!" For there is nothing that breathes without the Lord.

Inhaling and exhaling.

"Praise the Lord!"

We can no more hold our praise than we can hold our breath. To live is to praise God. Living is praying. We, however, are not usually aware of this. "Learning to pray" means in effect getting in touch with the basic character of our existence. When we pray we do not practice a religious ritual that is on the periphery of life. Rather, we move into the center of life. We become conscious of a process that is going on all the time, just as we are breathing all the time.

Prayer is the most natural thing in the world. Prayer seems strange to us only because we are alienated from our essential nature. People have always been blocking their capacity for prayer with the constructions of their minds and the pretensions of their hearts. But for us contemporary people the problem is intensified by the wonders of science. We are more impressed with our ability to sustain life than with the fact that there is life in the first place. Our problem is not our accomplishments but the attitude we take toward them. We view them as evidence of self-sufficiency and forget that it is the Lord who has "made us, and not we ourselves" (Ps. 100:3, marg.).

Nuclear overkill, environmental rape, and world starvation result from ignoring the psalmist's command to "let everything that breathes praise the Lord." Proposals to solve global problems are doomed unless we follow the psalmist's instruction. To many pragmatists this statement will sound like folly. They cannot understand why people would pray rather than act. They fail to perceive that our root problem is not our lack of action but our estrangement from the rest of the universe. We consider the world a machine to adjust and to rebuild as we see fit. But the psalmist views the world as a living reality that joins with us in the common praise of God.

The psalmist's perspective reorients our approach to action. We no longer operate as autonomous masters of an inanimate world. We understand that the world, like ourselves, is praising God. Action that violates the worshipful character of existence is abhorrent. The primary test for any particular action is: Does it "let everything that breathes praise the Lord"?—is it in harmony with the fundamental structure of the universe? We are currently discovering that to ignore this question is to commit suicide. It turns out that the psalmist is the real pragmatist. The psalmist is the one who is urging the only perspective that will let life endure.

People who praise God are realists. People who confine themselves to action are dreamy idealists. They live with the illusion that finite solutions without regard to the essential character of existence can remedy human problems. This is dangerous idealism because on the surface it sounds so reasonable while in fact it can cause great destruction.

Praising God is giving up idealism and becoming pragmatic. Praising God is tossing away the mumbo jumbo of technological arrogance and speaking the facts of faith. Praising God is abandoning the illusion of human control and embracing the truth of God's power.

Praise is not a burden. It does not demand adding another duty to life. Praise involves the recognition and acceptance of who we really are. When we are praising God we feel right about ourselves.

We claim rather than deny the most important truth of our lives. We experience a fundamental integrity of purpose and function, reason and action.

Praising God is like finding the right job after trying our hand in fields for which we were unsuited by either temperament or talent. Our minds come alive. Our imaginations function again. We settle at last into our proper calling.

Praise is discovering our vocation as breathing creatures. We leave behind our anguished private prayers and take our place in the worshiping congregation. We accept the job that perfectly matches our essential character as creations of God. We give up the foolish employment of pouring out excuses for our failure, our evil, and our insecurity. We turn from the flimsy products of human pride to the enduring goods of recognizing our dependence on God.

Praise is work, but it is glad work. It is using the raw materials of feeling, intellect, and strength on the one project for which they are most suited.

Praising God does not exhaust our interior resources but continually replenishes them. For praising God is a cyclical process. It is as important to the vitality of existence as the water and nitrogen cycles are to the continuance of the natural world.

God initiates the cycle by breathing into us the breath of life. We reciprocate with the breath of praise, which in turn comes back to us as renewed life. If we interrupt this process, we shall die as certainly as the natural world does when we violate its basic life cycles.

But if we nurture the cycle of praise, we nurture life itself. We clarify the mind and purify the heart. We feel the giddy gladness of living, and we join the psalmist in exclaiming: "Let everything that breathes praise the Lord!"

12

Exactly What
We Believe

Prayer is a journey. The point of departure is exactly how I feel. The destination is exactly what we believe. Prayer is traveling from me to us and from feeling to faith. Prayer's tour guide is the Psalter. It gives extensive information about our trip: Preparation. Getting started. What to see on the way. Our fellow travelers. Our destination.

Preparation. The psalms reveal that arrangements for our journey have already been made. God has taken the initiative and looked after every major matter. God has created the universe. God has fashioned people for a meaningful life. God has freed Israel. God has made a covenant. God maintains a continual interest in the world.

God's preparations are evident in every psalm. The allusions to the history of Israel and the creation of the world signify that prayer does not take place in the isolation of our lives. A unique experience may instigate a particular personal prayer, but we are never breaking the trail for the first time. God has prepared a way through life's wilderness. God has traveled ahead of us. This was clear to the Old Testament writers, and it is even clearer to Christians. When we pray in the face of death and temptation, we know that Jesus Christ has already passed this way.

Getting started. When we travel we are usually anxious that we may leave something behind. Something that we'll need on the first night away from home. We waste time and energy packing and repacking. Have I studied enough Scripture? Am I religious enough? How should I address God? The psalmists do not worry about these questions. They simply strike out on their trip. They travel toward God clothed in whatever experience, feeling, or object is immediately at hand: a close call, a need for forgiveness, a sense of gladness.

What to see on the way. There is much that we are apt to miss when we make our first trip. A woman who was a seasoned world traveler and noted for her exquisite pictures of people recalls a trip on which a man kept telling her to get ready for the next big sight. "You won't want to miss this one. Be sure to get a picture of it." All the time the woman occupied herself with the scenes of children and workmen and families. She knew that there was a hidden human beauty that would not be found in the most inspiring monuments, and she did not miss it by keeping her eyes peeled only for grandeur.

The psalmists instruct us not to look exclusively for glorious visions. Instead, they note the simple things. A hill. The first light of morning. A child upon a mother's breast. The sound of a flute. These are not diversions along the way. Through these ordinary things heaven is opened to us. We do not keep looking for God to "answer" us with some great sign. Rather, we hear God's voice and sense God's presence in the common things of life.

Our fellow travelers. We are not the only ones to take the journey of prayer. We may feel more comfortable starting out alone, but as soon as we catch a glimpse of our destination we want to share our wonder and delight. The psalmists do this over and over. They turn from themselves to the congregation of Israel. Grace, forgiveness, faith, praise—all must be shared to be relished to the full.

When people ask why they *ought* to participate in a life of Christian fellowship, they reveal that they have missed the real glory and joy of God. Corporate worship is our spontaneous desire when we have tasted the depths of God's presence. Private prayer impels us to public worship because it fills us with an exuberant readiness to share what we have found.

When our private prayer putters out, as it inevitably does at different times in life, then the congregation keeps us traveling on. We do not cancel out the rest of the trip and return home. We are committed to travel with this group. Just when our private interest is lagging, others—who before seemed to take no interest—are getting excited. We are sustained by their prayerful enthusiasm, just as before they were sustained by ours.

The more we travel with other people in prayer, the more we appreciate each other. They point out things we might have missed. We share insights that eluded them. We discover that our fundamental feelings and needs are the same. Prayer becomes the process of claiming our common humanity. We no longer think simply of "My God" but of "Our God." We no longer pray simply for "me." We pray for "us." Prayer becomes mutual concern.

Destination. We start from feeling and travel toward faith. Faith is not devoid of feeling. It often awakens the deepest emotions. However, our destination includes much more than "getting in touch with our feelings" or figuring out what we are "really like inside." We shall fade like the grass. We shall be turned back to dust and be swept away like a dream (Ps. 90:3ff.). The goal of our journey is something much more enduring than the passing show of ourselves.

We seek God. Not as an abstract principle nor as theological dogma. But God as the One who understands what we feel, yet is much greater than our inner state. We use our feeling and our experience to leap beyond ourselves.

Our destination defines our entire journey. The little details of getting started and losing our way vanish in the joy of arrival. Talk to a traveler who has visited something that he or she has always wanted to see. Bad food and mixed-up schedules are forgotten during the experience of finally being there. "I shall never forget the excitement of when I first laid my eyes on it."

So it is with the psalmists and ourselves when we pray from common experience. Whatever may have started us on our way, whatever difficulties we may have encountered, are left far behind in the gladness of finding that God is present. God cares! God understands! God loves! The affirmation that God "will redeem Israel from all his iniquities" (Ps. 130:8) obliterates the last trace of guilt that drove the psalmist to pray in the first place: "Out of the depths I cry to thee, O Lord!" (Ps. 130:1).

Psalm 130's pattern is repeated over and over. Anguish is lost in praise. Pain is forgotten in adoration. Guilt is buried in forgiveness. Feeling is transcended in faith. Self-preoccupation is lost in the presence of God. Every force that would destroy and alienate and scare us is vanquished. To put this in the most compact possible form: "Death is swallowed up in victory" (I Cor. 15:54). Prayer is resurrection! For prayer takes the reality of finite experience and transforms it into new life.

God revealed the power of resurrection by starting out with common objects that we could see and believe in: a carpenter's body, three nails, and a blood-soaked piece of wood. A scene of violence. Something that is absolutely credible from everything we know of human nature and from what we see on television. Then God transformed this finite, visible scene into something shatteringly different. New life. A person who is present with people in every setting and situation. A risen Lord.

Prayer follows the resurrection pattern. It starts from what we know—a close call, a collapsing nation, guilt, a thunderstorm. Then through the power of the Spirit these are transformed into faith and hope. We end up with new life.

The precise dynamics of the transformation are beyond analysis. Like our final resurrection, the resurrection of prayer is ultimately a "mystery" (I Cor. 15:51). Yet God has been gracious enough to supply us with the practical information that we need for realizing this mystery in our lives.

Let us then with the psalmists begin to pray from our common experience. Let us delay no longer with excuses that we do not know how or that we cannot find the right words. Let us trust that God will lead us from our immediate feelings to a lasting faith. As surely as God raised Christ from the dead, God will raise us from ourselves. Even if our first words are, "My God, my God, why hast thou forsaken me?" our final words will be, "Praise the Lord!"

13

Postscript

This book has distorted the psalms. That is how it may appear to students of the Psalter who are familiar with a more traditional scholarly approach.

Most commentaries begin their analysis of a psalm by classifying it according to form and function. For example, Psalm 74 is a community lament. It has the elements that are common to this type of psalm: a description of the immediate crisis (vs. 1–11); reflection on God's past acts of intervention (vs. 12–17); and a plea for the Lord's help now (vs. 18–23). Analyzing a psalm in this fashion is revealing. It makes clear the psalm's fundamental structure. It sometimes suggests the possible cultic use or origin of the psalm. It invites comparison of the psalm to similar literature from the surrounding cultures of the ancient Near East. All of this can help us to probe and to understand more precisely the meaning of a particular psalm.

However, people who turn to the Psalter for guidance in prayer are looking for something other than scholarly comprehension. The text is not an objective reality that stands independent of their need. Rather, they read a psalm hoping to find some vital experience that connects with their own existence.

Readers bring to the psalms what they have seen and felt and heard. This is why I have opened each chapter with a story. I am affirming the subjective expectations of those who think the psalms can illumine their common life.

My analysis of Psalm 74 opens with a story about a parishioner who feels that the world is collapsing. My intention is to locate an experiential bond between the psalmist and us. In the face of radical upheaval we need to pray to God, but we are not sure how to do it. The psalmist has already contended with this problem. He can start us praying when we cannot do it ourselves.

There are dangers in my approach. We may use the psalms like a Rorschach inkblot test and read into them whatever meaning we already have in our heads. The text will not interpret and reshape our experience, but we will interpret and reshape the text.

The same dangers, however, are present in an exclusively objective approach and may even be more dangerous than in the patently subjective distortions of piety. We may become so intrigued with the cultic and structural elements of a psalm that we fail to perceive its fundamental existential dynamics. A particular psalm's value may be reduced to confirming a theory of classification or lending support to the reconstruction of ancient worship.

What we are dealing with here is nothing less than the relationship between Biblical scholarship and the subjective appropriation of Scripture by a person of faith. This issue is always alive for any Christian who is intellectually honest and prayerfully devout. The confrontation becomes critical when such a person uses the Psalter as an aid to personal prayer. Which wins out:

Scholarly knowledge about a psalm, or an emotional reaction to the experience it captures?

A psalm's ancient liturgical usage, or its inner personal meaning?

A psalm's public proclamation, or its interior revelation?

The answer to this dilemma is to be found in the psalms themselves. They overcome the polarities of objective knowledge and subjective significance by working simultaneously at two levels: the psychological and the liturgical.

The psalms are characterized by psychological integrity. The psalmists are honest about what they feel. They may use certain forms in which to express themselves, but these forms never hide that it is flesh and blood who is calling to God. The psalmists' urgency and depth of feeling are undeniably present. If the psalms were simply mechanical formulas for dealing with God, they would lack the strong healing and pastoral powers for which they are treasured.

The psalms are also marked by liturgical integrity. The psalmists are faithful to the worshiping commuity—to its services, to its traditions, to its corporate needs. Time and again we have noted the movement from "I" to "we," from the private to the public. The psalmists may give vent to their most intense feelings, but these feelings do not cut them off from Israel's faith and worship. The psalmists are guided by the larger community. If the psalms were simply emotional outbursts, they would not be the potent resource for corporate worship which they are.

There is a reciprocal relationship between the psychological and the liturgical character of the psalms. Each benefits the other.

Effective worship resonates with the world of those who participate, and that is exactly what the psalms do. Their truthfulness to what people feel grabs the heart and pulses through the arteries. The psalms identify what it means to be human. They make worship an occasion for personal insight as well as divine revelation.

Because they take people's feelings seriously, the psalms open people to God. They do not ignore a person's internal state, as though God had no interest in humanity's common joys and fears! The psalms' psychological integrity makes them theologically powerful. Their subjective authenticity wins acknowledgment of their objective truth.

In a reverse manner, the psalms' liturgical integrity facilitates emotional release. The psalmist turns to a structure—a set of symbols and forms—that lets him face his inner turmoil. Without this structure, the psalmist would be drowned by the ocean of feeling that rolls within him.

When the psalmist mourns for the collapse of the nation, his grief is sharp but not debilitating. The psalmist has recourse to a lament, to a particular way of sharing grief with God. This form allows for the expression of feeling without becoming swallowed by it.

The reciprocal relationship between psychology and liturgy, feeling and form, self and community, experience and tradition is the psalms' greatest revelation about the nature of prayer. In prayer the subjective elements of our existence are identified and resolved through encounter with the transcendent truth of God.

Liturgy is an expression of belief in this truth. The union of psychological and liturgical elements signifies the interweaving of the self's peculiar experience with the reality of God. Prayer is the experience of the coherence of existence.

Prayer is problematic for modern people because the wholeness of life is no longer apparent. The atrophy of language, the exaltation of the self ("Do your own thing!"), and the absence of community symbols and common beliefs are all symptomatic of a fragmented culture.

Because there is no longer a supportive environment for prayer, as there was for the psalmists, prayer becomes exclusively private. It turns into an act of the solitary soul.

The prayer of an individual will always carry its peculiar inflection, but to reduce the human resources for prayer only to what each individual possesses is to cripple people's ability to pray. To address the One Eternal God appears an awesome task to the isolated self. How can I who am bone and tendon and muscle speak to God who is Spirit?

The psalmists could leap from earth to heaven because they knew they were not alone. Their nation's history, their community's worship, their common faith, and their fund of particular psalm types provided a context, a fundamental orientation that let them burst into prayer. Contrary to modern wisdom, form and convention do not block expression but facilitate it. They provide a way of shaping experience into meaningful prayer.

It is a pious illusion to believe that private prayer alone can heal the hurt of contemporary existence. The psalms reveal that authentic personal prayer requires a community of faith. Shared beliefs and common symbols give the strength that an individual lacks.

Our broken existence does not provide adequate support for authentic personal prayer. It is not enough to pray from common experience. We need to pray *with* someone else. That is why I have subtitled this book "Praying *with* the Psalmists." We need the comradeship of the psalmists because we can no longer draw strength for prayer from the culture.

There was a time in Western history when faith integrated life for the whole society. But all that remains of such a cultural belief is a threadbare tapestry, a mere suggestion of its former glory. Once it was a bold fabric woven from the strands of community experience and the revelations of God. Now it is worn and faded and hanging in the past like a medieval arras in a museum.

Our pluralistic society is not about to restore the faith of the past. Those who pray nowadays must look beyond the confines of contemporary culture for support and guidance.

Unfortunately, the church reflects the same fragmentation that characterizes the culture. Nowhere is this more apparent than in the chasm separating the pastoral use of Scripture from Biblical scholarship.

In the case of the psalms we experience the split whenever we are torn between our critical understanding of a text and our use of that text to minister to a modern situation. Of course, when the psalmists prayed, they were not thinking of automobile accidents, the turbulent 1960's, stereophonic celebrations, or Air Force brides. But if we cannot find a fundamental dynamic that runs through both modern phenomena and ancient experience, then we are bereft of the psalms as a resource for prayer. Humanly speaking, we are alone. Our culture provides no support, and worst of all, Scripture provides no support. All that the psalms reveal are ancient customs. We can classify them. We can speculate on how they were used. We can piece together the possible historical background. We can talk about their parallels in other religious literature. But we cannot use them to help us pray from our common experience.

Who will make the daring leaps between the psalmists and us? Who will risk distorting a text in order to put right a life? Is it to be only the pastor and never the critical commentator? Are the scholars to think their work done because they have fixed with certainty the meaning of each word and the original form and setting of the psalm? No, that is bad scholarship. It creates the gravest distortion of all by ignoring the heart of faith that pumps the blood of thought and feeling through the forms of praise and prayer.

Scholarship must not be abandoned, but must be fulfilled. It must ask about the existential as well as the formal structure of the psalms. What is the essential pattern of existence that lies behind the psalmist's particular experience? To raise this question is not to neglect the type or function or setting of a psalm. It is, rather, to move toward comprehending the psalmist's total situation.

When we feel the anguish of watching a nation collapse and simultaneously recognize that we are reading a lament, then we genuinely understand Psalm 74. For us, as for the psalmist, form and feeling blend into a unitary experience, and the word that God would speak to us sounds with equal power in both our heart and our head.

To recover an integrated vision of existence requires prayerful scholarship and scholarly prayer.

Prayerful scholarship means a mastery of Scripture that proceeds from a desire to examine the full meaning of a passage, its existential flesh as well as its historical skeleton.

So far, Biblical scholarship has approached Scripture like a physician who puts stock only in X-rays and lab reports and never gets around to asking the patient how he feels or where he hurts. We learn a lot about the theological metabolism of the Bible but know little about its soul.

Scholarly prayer means a life of personal devotion that roots itself in the critical study of Scripture as well as the interior notions of the self.

Too often, pious disciples distort faith in exactly the opposite direction from scholars. They approach Scripture like a physician who listens only to the patient and spends no time examining the X-rays and the lab reports. The end result is knowledge about the soul but not the body of God's word.

The psalmists overcome this split. They feel the pulse of their hearts while at the same time they know the anatomy of faith.

In the coherence of existence which the psalmists experience lies the power to heal our broken lives. It is time for the scholar and the prayerful disciple to embrace each other. If this union of thought and feeling, sophisticated theology and simple belief, does not become real in the church, then Christians will confirm the culture's chaos. But if like the psalmists we draw together the fractured pieces of our common life, our prayers shall be a witness to the world about the One in whom "all things hold together" (Col. 1:17).